The
INCREDIBLE
WOMEN
of the
ALL-AMERICAN GIRLS
PROFESSIONAL
BASEBALL
LEAGUE

The INCREDIBLE WOMEN of the ALL-AMERICAN GIRLS PROFESSIONAL BASEBALL LEAGUE

By Anika Orrock

Foreword by Jean Afterman

CHRONICLE BOOKS

SAN FRANCISCO

Library of Congress Cataloging-in-Publication Data available.

ISBN 978-1-4521-7364-1

Manufactured in China.

Cover design by Jessica Hische and Anika Orrock.

Interior design by Maggie Edelman.

10 9 8 7 6 5 4 3 2 1

Chronicle books and gifts are available at special quantity discounts to corporations, professional associations, literacy programs, and other organizations. For details and discount information, please contact our premiums department at corporatesales@chroniclebooks.com or at 1-800-759-0190.

Chronicle Books LLC
680 Second Street
San Francisco, California 94107

www.chroniclebooks.com

This book is dedicated to the women of the
All-American Girls Professional Baseball League, and
to all women and girls everywhere throughout time
who perpetuate the gift of possiblity by having the
grit and tenacity to stay true to themselves.

Foreword

By Jean Afterman

Barely twenty-five years after women gained the right to vote, young women and girls answered the call and took to diamonds all over the United States to play baseball. They came not only for sport and pleasure, but as professionals, to support their families and communities during a time of war. They came from cities and small towns, from farms and areas of industry. They followed a strict code, donning ladylike skirts and lipstick along with their mitts, and they barnstormed throughout the United States playing the peculiarly American game of baseball.

I was born and raised in the lovely city of San Francisco, California, where my life in baseball began in the bleachers of Candlestick Park. Since the end of 2001, I have been privileged to be the Assistant General Manager of the New York Yankees, a franchise that is historic, proud, timeless, and iconic. When you walked onto the playing field at the old Yankee Stadium, you could not help but hear the echo of the crowds from a hundred years past, and see visions of Yankee greats striding out onto the field. When we played our last game in the old Yankee Stadium in 2008, Yankees Captain Derek Jeter told the packed house: "We're relying on you to take the memories from this stadium and add them to the new memories we make at the new Yankee Stadium." Ten years in and the memories of those long ago times are ever present— memory is the engine that drives our baseball lives.

That sense of tradition, honor, and pride has been carried down the decades, from stadium to stadium, all of which is to say I have been witness to greatness and to history. I have met Major League Hall of Famers and ball players who have the Hall of Fame in their future. I have been privileged to be the third woman Assistant General Manager in Major League Baseball history, and alas, as of my writing this in 2019, I am the only woman currently holding the position. The New York Yankees are the only team in all of professional sports to have hired not one, but two female Assistant General Managers (myself and my predecessor, Kim Ng), which I feel is another achievement to be added to the long list of superlatives about my organization.

On a day during the 2018 season, I had the immense pleasure of coming into contact with women who blazed a trail across this country that young women are following to this day. In celebration of the 75th Anniversary of the All-American Girls Professional Baseball League (AAGPBL), we honored some of these great players in a pre-game ceremony on the field at Yankee Stadium. I was able to spend part of the day with these veterans — I laughed at their sense of humor, I was awed by their stories, and I felt a pull at my heart. Their stories are remarkable, and resonate today.

One player recounted to me a memory from shortly after her AAGPBL days, touring and playing baseball with Bill Allington's All-Stars. While barnstorming through Texas, the All-Stars heard that a Negro League team was in town, so they went over to challenge them to a game. The local sheriff got wind of this and showed up with other law enforcement to prevent the game from happening. When the sheriff threatened the woman personally, saying if she took the field, he would "throw her back across the border," she looked at him and said, "I don't see any border around here, so you better have a good arm!" In the end, the women stood up to the sheriff by refusing to leave and the game was played. Some things never seem to change, and we need women like these, now more than ever.

Sometimes coming into close contact with the past gives you a renewed sense of purpose for the future. It is my hope that this book about those extraordinary women of character and ability, *by* an extraordinary woman, brings them to life for a new generation, and that it encourages more girls and young women to follow their dreams and to admit no barriers to their own success.

During the 2017 season, I came to know Anika Orrock when someone gave me a thank you gift for a speaking engagement. It was one of her drawings inspired by the AAGPBL. I was captivated. Through the miracle of the internet, I located her, and likewise learned that her grandfather, Ray Orrock, had been a syndicated columnist in the San Francisco Bay Area as I was growing up, writing columns I had read when I was young. Kismet!

Within these pages, Anika has stitched together a remarkable panoply of the AAGPBL players' love, their longing, and their passion for the game of baseball. These are not only echoes from the past, but rich voices that need to be listened to today. As I think about the women of the AAGPBL, I am mindful of the quote about the dancing of Fred Astaire and Ginger Rogers. The story goes that Bob Thaves, a cartoonist for a Los Angeles newspaper, drew a cartoon for his "Frank and Ernest" series as follows: Frank and Ernest are shown gazing at a billboard announcing a Fred Astaire film festival. The caption reads: "Sure he was great, but don't forget that Ginger Rogers did everything he did . . . backwards and in high heels."

In these pages, you will learn how the AAGPBL came to be, that the girls and women of the league played just as hard as the men, but did it in short skirts and makeup (this was the 1940s and 1950s, after all). Hollywood gave these women a lovely, albeit somewhat fictional, treatment, but these women have real stories to tell, real voices to be heard. They remind us that women still need to fight for equality in the world. And they remind us of our own lives, how we fell in love with the game of baseball at a very young age, and like the veterans of the AAGPBL, we love it just as much as we ever did.

Introduction
The Warm-Up

"There's no crying in baseball!"

As a lifelong fan of the game, I can safely say this iconic adage from the classic 1992 movie *A League of Their Own* just isn't true.

I recall several summer evenings as a kid listening to San Francisco Giants baseball games on the radio with my grandparents, when at least one of us would burst into tears at some point during the broadcast. This aspect of baseball really only gets worse with adulthood.

If you grow up loving baseball, you know that crying has as much place in the sport as hot dogs or Cracker Jack. As kids, we cry over the devastation of a loss or the elation of a win. As we get older, it's the beautiful moments that get us; our own stories of triumph and defeat are reflected in these moments, and we just can't help but feel nostalgic. Baseball itself is positively rich with stories and nostalgia.

Sure, it is only a game, but for the better part of a century, baseball was *the* common language in America—something everyone from everywhere could talk about at the butcher or the barbershop. Its stories are stitched into the national identity, containing figures as folkloric as John Henry or Annie Oakley. For someone like me who thrives on storytelling, baseball is a bottomless well of inspiration.

My personal baseball lineage can be traced as far back as my great-grandfather, Raymond "Bust 'em" Orrock. Nicknamed for his powerful hitting, Bust 'em played second base and later managed the Vallejo ball club, one of the many city organizations popular in Northern California before the major leagues came west. Bust 'em's son and my grandfather, Ray Orrock, played a bit in college but found his calling as a cartoonist and a writer, remaining a vocal fan of the game (along with my even more vocal grandmother) for the rest of his life.

With a few exceptions, athletic prowess in my family pretty much ends with Bust 'em Orrock. Those of us who tried playing baseball in a somewhat serious capacity quickly realized that our love for the game very much outweighed our on-field skill. Therefore, in my family we demonstrate our reverence for baseball by not playing it.

This is why I draw and write about baseball, and due to a fortuitous friendship with Hall of Fame broadcaster for the San Francisco Giants, Jon Miller, I've had the joyful privilege of drawing from various perches in numerous ballparks.

A few years ago, while flipping through stacks of these drawings, I began to realize something: apart from a few sketches of fans in the ballpark, there was not a single drawing of a woman or a girl. Being a woman myself (who, incidentally, was once a girl), this was a somewhat startling observation. From a creative standpoint, I had clearly been depriving myself of artistic diversity! But as a fan of baseball and its history, I was suddenly bursting with questions I had not previously considered.

Girls play softball. That was certainly my only ball playing option growing up. Softball is a great sport, but softball and baseball are not the same. I wanted to play baseball, but seeing as how I lacked the athletic chutzpah to adapt to softball, I happily took to cartooning and writing instead. But what about girls who want to play baseball? What about baseball writers and managers and umpires and scouts? What about *athletes*? What about *women in baseball*?

I became obsessed with this largely invisible aspect of baseball history. Certainly there were incredible women among the ranks of baseball legends. I began my journey by opening Netflix to the one good story I already knew of: Penny Marshall's film *A League of Their Own*, inspired by the All-American Girls Baseball League (now known as the All-American Girls Professional Baseball League).*

As I would learn after years of intensive research and player interviews, Tom Hanks's famous line "There's no crying in baseball!" is not the film's only falsehood. But a good story requires a healthy sprinkle of Hollywood for the big screen, and I'm not alone in thinking that *A League of Their Own* is a really great movie.

Penny Marshall made the existence of the All-American Girls Baseball League indelible. She gave the league's story to everyone, while giving new life to its former players. Without *A League of Their Own*, this book would likely not exist; the spirit it captured inspired many— including at least one baseball-loving cartoonist—to learn more about the league, as well as numerous other meaningful chapters in baseball history that have been glossed over and forgotten.

But there is so much more to the real story of the All-American Girls Baseball League than can be gleaned from a two-hour film, and who better to tell it than the incredible women who lived it? Times have changed for women in America, but still we haven't seen anything like it; a professional league for women's baseball has not existed in America since the All-American League folded in 1954.

The stories in this book, shared by former All-Americans and their family members, provide a pure, wonderful, and honest way to view the past, present, and future of women in America and in baseball. They illuminate racial and gender injustices we have yet to overcome and show us ways to be better. They also offer us an opportunity to visit an incredibly unique moment in history that continues to reveal its significance as it ripples through time.

I hope you enjoy *The Incredible Women of the All-American Girls Professional Baseball League* the way you might enjoy a scrapbook you've just unearthed from an old trunk in your great-aunt's attic. At the very least, I sincerely hope you enjoy reading this delightful collection of memories and stories half as much as I've enjoyed recording them.

Play ball!

* The All-American Girls Professional Baseball League (AAGPBL), as it has been known since the 1980s, existed under a variety of names during its eleven-season run. For most of its existence, it was known as the All-American Girls Baseball League (AAGBBL) and was popularly referred to by that name throughout its many official changes. For this reason (and to avoid confusion), the league will consistently be referred to in this book as the All-American Girls Baseball League (AAGBBL). Additionally, players included in this book are referred to by the names they used while playing in the league.

"December 7th, 1941–a date which will live in infamy . . ."

Just one day after the sudden and deliberate attack on Pearl Harbor, President Franklin D. Roosevelt would address Congress and country, and within hours the United States of America would officially enter World War II. Little more than twenty years out of the previous war, reluctant Americans divided by the idea of foreign involvement were united by the darker prospect of Hitler's ideology and the rapidly expanding hostilities of Nazi Germany and its Axis partners in Japan and Italy.

The nation mobilized swiftly. Rubber, food, and gas rations were on. Victory gardens were planted; war bonds purchased; scrap metal, tires, and cooking fat were collected and recycled into ammunition and aircrafts.

As civilians gave their all on the home front, millions of newly enlisted Americans battled abroad. Within the year, nearly every major industry would convert to war production, and military manpower would more than double. The demand for "all hands on deck" necessitated the service and skill of every citizen, regardless of race or gender. Despite discrimination and military segregation, over 2.5 million valiant African American men registered for the draft, and for the first time, within their own branches of the US military, women would have the opportunity to serve their country in an official capacity.

Women would also be needed on the front lines at home, filling labor positions vacated by male recruits and stepping into new, nontraditional positions created by wartime production. Millions of women who had never worked outside the home soon constituted over 30 percent of the American workforce, rarely earning more than 50 percent of their male counterparts' wages.

While it was a new and different battle, memories of the wartime past were not so distant. Mobilization efforts during the First World War had required all men with "nonessential" occupations to take up war-related jobs or be drafted, and during that time, baseball had been deemed nonessential.

Uncertain about the future of the game and its role in World War II America, baseball commissioner Kenesaw M. Landis solicited President Roosevelt's advice. In what would become known as the Green Light Letter, Roosevelt replied with his "personal and not an official point of view," expressing his feeling that "it would be best for the country to keep baseball going. There will be fewer people unemployed and everybody will work longer hours and harder than ever before. And that means that they ought to have a chance for recreation and for taking their minds off their work even more than before."

Of course, military manpower being the higher priority, Roosevelt added, "As to the players themselves, I know you agree with me that the individual players who are of active military or naval age should go, without question, into the services."

And that was that. America's national pastime was decidedly essential for maintaining morale. Baseball would continue!

But if no men were around to play it, would anyone pay to see it?

"PK Wrigley, owner of the Chicago Cubs; Branch Rickey, now president of the Brooklyn Dodgers; and Warren Giles of the Cincinnati Reds had a desperation meeting. They reminded each other that more than 1 million girls in the land were playing softball. Most of them were playing a semi professional sort of game. . . . These games were attracting a great many fans. Wrigley and Ricky and Giles went to some of the games. They were astonished at the skill of the girls and amazed at the violent enthusiasm of the customers. They decided that the girls game might be fully professionalized, that a big-time league might be set up as a sort of cushion to keep baseball alive until the big leagues could recover from the depredations of the war."

Morris Markey, "Hey Ma, You're Out!," *McCall's*, September 1950

Though he was more business than baseball, Philip K. Wrigley was above all patriotic. A former navy man himself, the chewing gum magnate ceased all production of premium products during World War II and shipped every remaining stick to the soldiers overseas. With imported ingredient supplies cut off, Wrigley, not wanting to sacrifice the quality of his bestselling brands, devised a domestically sourced, temporary substitute. Sure, it was openly advertised as inferior, but Orbit gum would keep Wrigley manufacturing moving; it would do the job.

Baseball, Wrigley's *other* enterprise, would be no exception to his wartime business model. Just as Wrigley had inherited his industrialist father's keen business sense and well-known chewing gum corporation, so had he inherited ownership of the major league Chicago Cubs baseball club. With premium products—that is, players—unavailable during the war, Wrigley would source an abundant and sufficient substitute: women. Unlike Orbit gum, however, Wrigley suspected that this substitute wouldn't be inferior at all, and he had big ambitions for developing a fresh, long-lasting sport.

Known for being fiscally conservative in other ways, Wrigley spared no expense when it came to marketing. The devout ad man was perpetually pitching Cubs baseball to Chicagoans for the "fun, and the healthfulness" of the game, "the sunshine and the relaxation." Winning or losing was irrelevant when it came to getting "the public to see ball games." (Incidentally, one could claim that the Cubs' 71-year slump was due to Wrigley's stingy player budget, rather than the fabled Curse of the Billy Goat.)

Something about Roosevelt's rationale resonated with Wrigley. By establishing the non-profit All-American Girls Softball League, Wrigley would fill "the need for additional recreation in towns busy with war defense." Keeping the business of baseball afloat would double as Wrigley's patriotic duty; it would do the job.

Unable to get a single major-league executive on board apart from Brooklyn's Branch Rickey, Wrigley bankrolled $100,000 of his own money, made Rickey a trustee, appointed former Cubs Assistant General Manager Ken Sells as president, and put his primary ad agent, Arthur Meyerhoff, to work sending scouts all over the United States and Canada in search of skilled ball slingers and stick swingers!

SPORT

Page Seventeen

The Times

day, May 3, 1943

EBALL

Wrigley Sinks $100,000 In Girls Softball Loop For Defense

rs Have Poor
ing Now In
nal Race

Four Team Loop Will Be Formed;
More Than 100 Players Signed

Wisconsin Daily Tribune

Swamp Dodgers; Giants Nip

Girls Softball League Spons

Wrigley To Glamorize Mora

Wrigley's Interests Pay Top Players

Sports

SALT LAKE CITY, UTAH
THURSDAY, MAY 27, 1943

BOX

Girls Professional
League Shares Us
Cubs Park

Experiment This Year Girls Sof
Plan Major League In 1944

Some of the young women who would try out for Wrigley's new league had experience playing organized softball. A good many of them, however, had never even played softball, let alone on a formal team. Regardless, nearly every woman who became an All-American grew up the only girl playing hardball with the boys in sandlots, streets, pastures, and parks, with no fancy uniforms or equipment and rarely enough players to fill the field.

"We're talking about the nineteen-forties. Individual sports were only for those elite families that had money and could have private lessons. Baseball was one of those things. . . . Every small town had a baseball team. There were enough remnants so you could play with a limited amount of space, a limited amount of equipment and still have a very good time."

Lois Youngen, catcher, 1951-54

"As soon as I would get up in the morning as a kid, I was all ready to go out and play ball."

Ann "Pee Wee" Meyer, shortstop, 1944

"Mother never said no as long as she knew where I was. She let me go right along [with] the boys. See, I grew up in an era where there were few opportunities for girls."

Mary "Prattie" Pratt, pitcher, 1943-47

"My mother thought that thing that was hanging from my right hand was part of my anatomy because that's how often it was there."

Jean "Cy" Cione, pitcher, first base, outfield, 1945-54

"My mother died when I was seventeen months old, so I never knew my mother; my brothers and sisters actually raised me. My youngest brother was nine years older than I was . . . and he set me to throwing. If he ever wanted to go out and play ball, he had to take me or else he couldn't go. They would stick me out in the outfield, but eventually I would work up to playing in the infield. I played ball as long as I can remember. It was my brothers that taught me to play ball."

Vivian "Kelly" Kellogg, first base, 1944-50

"I had an older brother that had a paper route. I would help him on his paper route to earn money, so I was the one who always would come up with bats and balls and the equipment. So if the boys wanted to play ball or any sport, be it football, basketball, they had to come get me first. So I was never left out."

Mary Moore, second base, 1950-52

C'MON, MARY!

"My brother never liked the fact that he wouldn't be picked before me. I had these trophies in the kitchen—my mother had them up—and his friends would come over and they would say, 'What did you get the trophy for?' My brother would say, 'They're my sister's.' "

Grace Piskula, outfield, 1944

"The boys came down to my house and they told me they didn't want me on the team anymore because the other towns' teams and kids were laughing at us because we had a girl on the team. It took them about a week before they came trudging back down and asked me to join 'em again because they had lost two games and they wanted me back on the team."

Lois Youngen

"Christmas, when I was about twelve years old, I asked for a baseball glove and my mother told me that girls don't get baseball gloves and I said, 'Then I don't want anything for Christmas—if I can't have a glove, I don't want anything.' So needless to say, my dad bought me a good glove."

Norma "Hitch" Whitney, second base, 1949-50

"My father, who was an avid, avid baseball fan, took me along to a game when I was about four years old and I fell in love with the game of baseball. When anybody asked me afterward, 'What are you going to do when you grow up?' I said, 'I'm going to play professional baseball!' not knowing there was such a thing anywhere in the country. . . . I had this dream. I never gave up on the dream and my classmates [in] high school kept saying, 'Salty, now what are you going to do when you graduate?' I'd say, 'I'm going to play professional baseball!' And I'm sure some of them laughed in my face, some of them maybe behind my back. They probably thought I'd lost it because as I say, nobody around here knew that such a thing existed anywhere."

Sarah Jane "Salty" Sands, right field, catcher, 1953–54

"I knew nothing about girls playing baseball. I thought I was the only one in the whole wide world that played baseball, of course with the boys. One morning, my father was reading the Sunday paper and he called me from the other room, 'Dolly!' he said, 'There's tryouts this afternoon for girls' baseball!' I said, *'Girls'* baseball?!'"

Dolly Niemiec, second base, third base, 1948–52

"When I walked in, I was stunned . . . to see all these other girls my age throwing the ball like I did, swinging, running, sliding—and I thought, 'Where did all these gals come from?!'"

Dolly Niemiec

"I thought I was pretty good back home, and I was. But then I got to spring training and I saw all the other girls playing and I thought 'wow.' I was a little fish in a big pond."

Sue Parsons, infield, outfield, pitcher, 1953-54

"I never played on a girls team, ever. I never played softball. I played only with the boys and men—grown men—so I never played with the girls. I figured, how hard could *that* be? Until I saw that first day [of tryouts], and then I realized how hard it could be. These girls [could] play ball."

Wilma "Briggsie" Briggs, outfield, first base, 1948-54

Hundreds upon hundreds of young women from all over the United States and Canada showed up for tryouts in several major cities. Those who made the initial cut traveled to Wrigley Field, where they reported for spring training on May 17, 1943. For many of these women, the journey to Chicago would be their first trip away from home and family.

NATIONAL
INNING
1 2 3 4 5 6 7 8 9

UMPIRES
PLATE 1ST 2ND 3RD

AMERICAN
INNING
1 2 3 4 5 6 7 8 9

BATTER

BALL   STRIKE

OUT

VIS   HITS   CUBS

"I don't think I slept much that first night on that train and the first sun-up I looked out and saw the wonderful rolling hills of Wisconsin go by and it is a memory etched in my mind forever, those wonderful rolling hills and green grass. . . . I was a little bit nervous about everything. . . . When we had breakfast on the train I just didn't even know what to order because I had never been out. Seeing the waiter with this white towel over one arm and a silver coffee pot in the other hand, I was just baffled by it all. It was just overwhelming to me, but . . . I guess most of the girls going were in the same position as I was."

Audrey "Dimples" Haine, pitcher, 1944-51

"[My family] didn't have any money, so that was my very first trip outside of California. They met me at the train and they took me to a hotel. . . . I had never been by myself, so I pushed the dresser up against the door and got me four baseballs and a bat and dared anybody to come in my room."

Maybelle Blair, pitcher, 1948

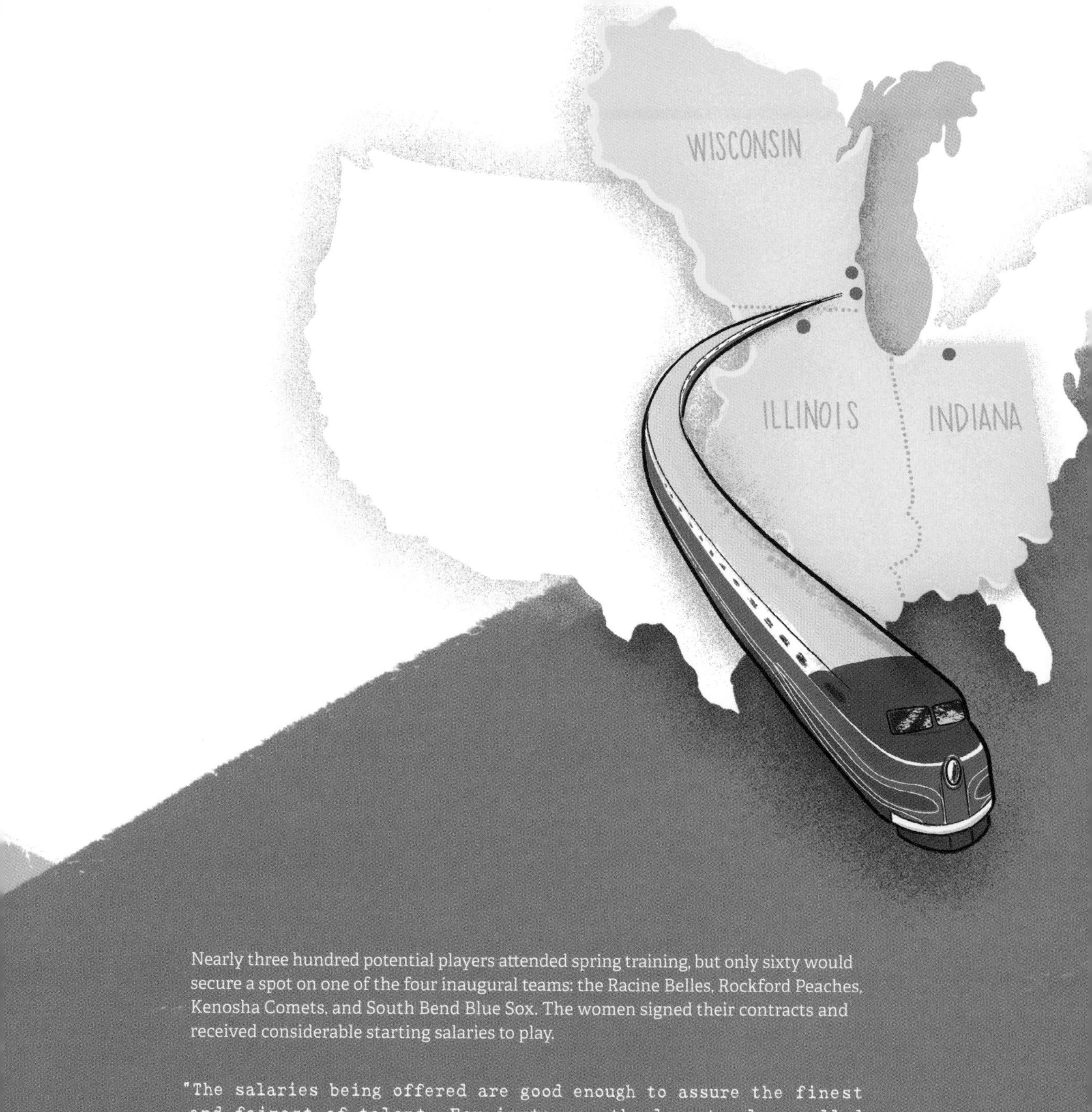

Nearly three hundred potential players attended spring training, but only sixty would secure a spot on one of the four inaugural teams: the Racine Belles, Rockford Peaches, Kenosha Comets, and South Bend Blue Sox. The women signed their contracts and received considerable starting salaries to play.

"The salaries being offered are good enough to assure the finest and fairest of talent. For instance, the lowest salary called for in a current contract is S45 a week, more than the average stenographer or factory girl gets, and far above the pay of the average Class D minor leaguer. The best salary is S85 a week, comparing favorably with the pay received by players in the top minor leagues. And in usual baseball style the girls get all their expenses paid while they're on the road."

Gene F. Hampson, *The Courier-News*, May 25, 1943

Though some recruits signed on as young as fifteen years old, most were over eighteen and well into their twenties, but that didn't exactly mean they could run home and pack their bags. Most women of the time lived at home until they were married, and while a solo train trip to Chicago was one thing, parents were reluctant to see their daughters travel around the country unsupervised for an entire season.

"I was about eighteen and my mother said, 'You're not going.' I was a senior in high school, trying to earn money for school, so I called [my old softball coach] and asked him to come over, and he said to my mother, 'Where [else] could she earn fifty dollars a week plus two-fifty a day for spending money?' My mother couldn't answer that. I wasn't earning that kind of money even at Schuster's [department store] or even in the defense plants soldering canteens! So they let me go."

Grace Piskula

Hesitant though they might have been, many parents appreciated the idea that their daughters would be earning good money—often more than their own fathers—and they also found peace of mind knowing their girls would reside in the homes of local families, and that every team would be accompanied by a female chaperone, along with a famous former major-leaguer for a coach. The war may have given ladies a leg up in the workforce, but the idea of women traveling and playing ball for a living was still unusual, to say the least.

"Even though I was of age, you still waited for your parent's permission to do these crazy things, because a girl playing baseball was crazy."

Mary Lou "ML" Studnicka,
pitcher, 1951-53

The 108-game inaugural season of the All-American Girls Softball League commenced with a Sunday doubleheader in South Bend on May 30, 1943, with the hometown Blue Sox facing down the rambunctious Rockford Peaches. They may have called it softball, but Wrigley and his men redesigned the game to be similar to baseball by allowing leadoff running and base stealing. In addition, pitchers would start their windup with one foot on the rubber, not two as in softball. The softball-standard thirty-five-foot distance between pitcher and home plate would be stretched to forty, and just as in baseball, nine players would take the field instead of softball's ten. This would be just the beginning of the league's speedy transition into full-fledged hardball.

"Revolutionary softball rules have been adopted to speed up play, and each team will leave its girls arrayed in pink, blue, green or yellow uniforms with three-quarter-length flair skirts."

Escanaba Daily Press, May 1, 1943

"The first time I put that uniform on, I cried . . . because it was never a dream to become a professional ball player. The dream was to survive, the dream was to do the best you can in whatever you do. It was like winning. This was my own kind of winning. I kind of stood there for a little bit after I was dressed and I said, 'Ah, this is it, this is it!' and I never forgot that."

Jacqueline "Jackie" Mattson, catcher, 1950–51

If there was one thing Wrigley knew well, it was how to sell. And if he was going to sell the public on a women's sporting spectacle in 1943, it would have to be exceptionally feminine. Women were essential to the war effort, but with conventional gender roles suddenly askew, there was growing social anxiety about the "unfeminine" female. Only a handful of competitive sports were "ladylike" enough to be widely accepted by society, and baseball wasn't one of them.

Wrigley's All-Americans would be dignified, displaying "the highest ideals of womanhood," starting with the uniform. Wrigley assigned his brilliant art director, Otis Shepard, to the task of fashioning the league's look. Drawing inspiration from the feminine frocks of figure skating and field hockey, Shepard collaborated with Wrigley's wife, Helen, and the league's first signed player, softball star Ann Harnett, to design a polished, pretty, and professional uniform that would set the All-Americans apart.

"No pants wearing, tough-talking female soft-baller will play on any of our four teams."

Ken Sells, league president, 1943-44. *Cincinnati Enquirer*, May 17, 1943

"Every effort is made to select girls of *ability*, real or potential, and to develop that ability to its fullest power. But no less emphasis is placed on femininity, for the reason that it is more dramatic to see a feminine-type girl throw, run and bat than to see a man or boy or a masculine-type girl do the same things. *The more feminine the appearance of the performer, the more dramatic her performance.* The highest possible standard of femininity-with-skill is, therefore, the aim of all administrative regulations adopted by the All-American League."

All-American Girls' Baseball League Rule Book

"The league makes a strong point of femininity. . . . The girls are not playing men's ball, are not trying to compete with men but are attempting to establish their own game. . . . They [shouldn't] be looked upon as freaks or anomalies simply because they are playing ball."

Robert Sullivan, "Who Said Girls Couldn't Play Baseball?," *Sunday News,*
July 4, 1948

"The costumes? Girls are not hired like chorus girls. They're hired for their playing, but the league directors were smart enough to devise costumes that are comfortable, allowing freedom of movement, and yet give rise to statements frequently heard as fans leave the fields: 'They lost . . . But they're cute.'"

Muskegon Lassies 1948 Yearbook

"If you look at the original uniform it's got like three yards of material in it. It's got all kinds of extra skirt. . . . You try to bend over and pick up a ground ball, you've got mostly skirt and no ball! They wanted us to keep it cinched in so it looked like we had a waistline, you know? Have you ever tried to catch with your arms and your dress tries to go up in the air? It's practically impossible. We would loosen everything when no one was watching, you know, we'd loosen this decorative belt that we had, which didn't serve any real purpose except being decorative."

Lois Youngen

"The girls wear no more cumbersome equipment and uniform than necessary, for comfort and speed."

Palladium-Item and Sun-Telegram, May 15, 1949

"We had no batting helmets, so if you got hit in the head, you got hit in the head, you know? We wore men's equipment. Our bats were men's bats, I couldn't find a bat that was small enough around. I think I probably would have been a pretty good hitter if I ever could have found a bat. The playing of the game was made a little difficult because of the fact that there was nothing much out there."

Lois Youngen

"I hit a lot of home runs and I was a long-ball hitter because I didn't like sliding in the short skirts. I always made sure [to] get a single, a double, a triple, or a home run. I wanted to make sure I would get to that base without sliding."

Catherine "Horsey" Horstman, infield, pitcher, catcher, 1951–54

"I had ambivalent feelings about the uniforms. . . . They were attractive and appealing, and many of the girls looked great in them. They were very feminine, and you could do the job—most of the time. But because I did attempt to steal bases, I did a lot of sliding, and the uniform didn't offer that much protection. I spent most of the season with strawberries on both legs. And, believe me, you never thought twice about sliding—you were being paid to play."

Shirley Jameson, outfield, 1943–46

"I came out with the catcher just before the game started, to warm up, and I was black and blue and purple and green. . . . My mother's sitting up in the stands with our chaperone and she sees [me] and she says, 'My god, you would think she would wash her legs!'"

Mary Lou Studnicka

"When you got a strawberry, of course, you'd go in the dugout and the chaperone would pour merthiolate on it, and your teammates would gather around and give you the fan—then she'd patch you up and send you back out onto the field."

Dolly Niemiec

"If you didn't play, there was somebody waiting to take your spot, so if you wanted to stay in the game, you played hurt."

Mary Lou Studnicka

"Believe me, you haven't lived until you've slid on skin."

Doris "Sammye" Sams, outfield, pitcher, 1946-53

"You know [the movie] said, 'There's no crying in baseball,' but I have to say, we wouldn't have thought to cry. I never saw a woman cry there ever. . . . You didn't think of it until after you slid. . . . You could hardly get up, but you took it, you toughened. . . . [We were] taking pain and learning to take pain, you're not born taking it."

Toni Palermo, shortstop, 1949-50

"You either played in that uniform or you went home, and I sure as heck wasn't about to go home."

Sarah Jane Sands

"The worst part was when you had your period, ooooohhh boy. Sometimes that became really grueling, you know what I mean? It wasn't a reason [not to play]. You just had to play through it. And wash a lot of underpants."

Eleanor "Ellie" Moore, pitcher, first base, 1950-54

"Very few of the players suffer undue disturbance at the monthly period, and many play the whole season without missing a game. They play all out. They get hurt in collisions. They have pulled muscles and Charley horses and spike cuts and bruises. But it is a rare thing for a girl to whimper over her pain or ask to be taken out of the game."

Morris Markey, "Hey Ma, You're Out!," *McCall's*, September 1950

"Tiby Eisen slides home with a run and a nicely bruised leg! Better a bruise than long pants, eh gals?"

U-I News newsreel, May 1950

Presenting the players as tough but feminine was certainly satisfying to the general public. Arthur Meyerhoff, Wrigley's marketing master, took charge of publicity and made sure there was plenty of it, both on the local level and in national newsreels, papers, and periodicals. With the first press release, however, came plenty of skepticism.

"There's going to be many barbed jests tossed at the Chicago Cubs as a result of their recently announced plan to promote a professional girls' softball team at Wrigley field."

Tommy Devine, *Tampa Tribune*, February 12, 1943

Meyerhoff campaigned to convince the critics. This sensational new league would wow crowds with surprising skill as well as femininity. But before the league's skill was made apparent, the press would have a field day with the feminine angle.

"A new league where a slim figure
will be as important as a fat batting
average opens Sunday. . . . The
girls will watch their diet, too.
Outmoded is the cry to pass the
potatoes. It's 'hand me the powder-
puff, dearie.'"

Jayne Miller, *Freeport Journal-Standard*, May 28, 1943

"You know getting a check for playing
baseball . . . I was just thrilled to death.
And I had never really had a real steak,
so the first thing I did was to go out
and order a big T-bone steak. I can just
almost taste it! I remember how excited I
was to have my first steak."

Jeneane "Lefty" DesCombes, pitcher, right field,
1953–54

"Each player who steps up to the plate
will be as trim as a ballet dancer
in her short-skirted pastel uniform.
Every curl will be in place, her
lipstick on precisely, and a tsk! tsk!
to the girl who hits a homer while her
face is shiny."

Jayne Miller, *Freeport Journal-Standard*, May 28, 1943

On-field aptitude was given priority over appearance when it came to selecting players, as Meyerhoff and Wrigley determined it was far easier to glamorize a good athlete than teach a clumsy stunner how to swing. They hired the school of world-renowned cosmetics maven Helena Rubenstein to conduct spring training charm courses. Players were also given beauty guides and makeup kits, as well as demonstrations in decorum.

"She taught us how to put on a coat and how to go up and down the stairs."

Betsy "Sockum" Jochum, outfield, first base, pitcher, 1943–48

"How to cross our legs and not to pile our dishes up when we went out."

Mary Pratt

"Well, how do you walk down the steps with a book on your head and a charley horse? It's bad enough with just the book on your head."

Jacqueline Mattson

"How to sit, how to do [everything] . . . education I never had in my life being on the farm, you know."

Ann Meyer

"And we each got a make-up kit. *That* was put away."

Betsy Jochum

YOUR ALL-AMERICAN GIRLS BASEBALL LEAGUE BEAUTY KIT

SHOULD ALWAYS CONTAIN THE FOLLOWING:

Cleansing Cream

Lipstick

Rouge—Medium

Cream Deodorant

Mild Astringent

Face powder for Brunette

Hand Lotion

Hair Remover

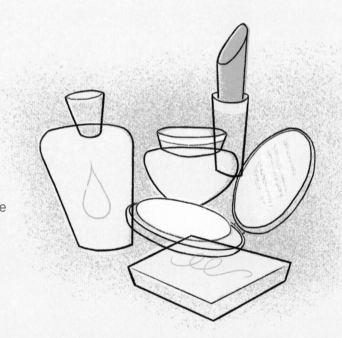

Suggested Beauty Routine

AFTER THE GAME

Remember, the All-American girl is subjected to greater exposure through her activities on the diamond, through exertion in greater body warmth and perspiration, through exposure to dirt, grime and dust and through vigorous play to scratches, cuts, abrasions and sprains. This means extra precaution to assure all the niceties of toilette and personality. Especially "after the game," the All-American girl should take time to observe the necessary beauty ritual, to protect both her health and appearance. Here are a few simple rules that should prove helpful and healthful "after the game."

"The Eyes are the Windows of the Soul"

The eyes indicate your physical fitness and therefore need your thoughtful attention and care. They bespeak your inner most thoughts—they reflect your own joy of living—or they can sometimes falsely bespeak the listlessness of mind and body. Perhaps no other feature of your face has more to do with the impression of beauty, sparkle and personality which you portray.

A simple little exercise for the eyes and one which does not take much time can do much to strengthen your eyes and add to their sparkle and allure. Turn your eyes to the corner of the room for a short space of time, then change to the other corner. Then gaze at the ceiling and at the floor alternately. Rotating or rolling your eyes constitutes an exercise and your eyes will repay you for the attention that you give to them.

There are also vitamins prescribed for the care of the eyes. Drink plenty of water and eat plenty of vegetables. We all know well that the armed forces found carrots a definite dietary aid to eyesight. Use a good eyewash frequently and for complete relaxation at opportune moments, lie down and apply an eye pad to your eyes for several minutes.

"[The beauty school instructors] told us stuff like, 'There are two eyebrows, not one,' and that stuck. . ."

Rose "Rosie" Folder, outfield, pitcher, 1944

"'I've been playing ball for over 12 years, [Terrie Davis] confided. 'I never had a scratch or bruise. So what happens? The first time I came up to bat here at Wrigley Field, I pop a foul tip. Bang! Down comes the ball right on my eye. Just look at the shiner.' Her black eye, however, wasn't as noticeable as she made out. Sells had sent her to a beauty operator who laid on grease paint and powder."

Jayne Miller, *Freeport Journal-Standard,* May 28, 1943

> **"Lipstick on every day all the time ... either wear it or you get fined! Five dollars and then ten dollars and then twenty dollars and then suspension, you were out!"**
>
> Catherine Horstman

"The plate umpire has conferred with the team captains. The diamond is ready. The home team begins its rush from the dugout—But, wait. They stop short. It seems the right fielder hasn't finished applying lipstick. That's a rule."

Sport Life, September 1951

Mouth

Every woman wants to have an attractive and pleasing mouth. As you speak, people watch your mouth and you can do much, with a few of the very simplest tools, to make your mouth invitingly bespeak your personality. Your beauty aids should, of course, include an appropriate type of lipstick and a brush. They should be selected with consideration and care.

With your lipstick, apply two curves to your upper lip. Press your lips together. Then, run your brush over the lipstick and apply it to your lips, outlining them smoothly. This is the artistic part of the treatment in creating a lovely mouth.

Caution: Now that you have completed the job, be sure that the lipstick has not smeared your teeth. Your mirror will tell the tale, and it is those little final touches that really count. . . .

45

Speech

"*You know she is a lady as soon as she opens her mouth.*"
The first requirement for charm of speech is a pleasing voice.
A low voice, instead of a high-pitched voice, is always most
pleasing. Making yourself heard is also most desirable.
Speak out clearly and enunciate properly.

Etiquette

Emily Post says that "charm cannot exist without good
manners." You do not have to have manners that follow
particular rules but the continued practice of kind and
friendly impulses, a kind, proper and courteous approach,
cannot help but add to your personality and give you a
big advantage in dealing with your every day contacts.
Here are some simple suggestions that will help you in
your development of a pleasing personality on and off
the playing field.

"Wonderful umpire, Barney Ross . . . but I was pitching to this girl who wasn't the best hitter and he called a strike a ball. Of course my catcher was yelling at him and I said, 'Barney, I want to tell you something,' and he said, 'Yes, Lou?' and I said, 'You are going blind!'

He said, 'Lou, I want to tell you something. You go back to that mound and I'll show you how blind I'm getting.'"

Louise "Lou" Arnold, pitcher, 1948–52

Introductions

Always acknowledge and always make an introduction in a pleasant and correct way. A man is always presented *to* a lady, such as: "Miss Young, may I present Mr. Smith" or "Miss Young, may I introduce Mr. Smith." Under all possible circumstances the reply to an introduction is "How do you do?" Well bred people do not say: "Pleased to meet you" but when it is actually true, you can say: "I am VERY glad to meet you." When a gentleman is introduced to a lady, she smiles, bows lightly and says: "How do you do."

The Baseball Fan

There is an old saying that "the customer is always right." This, in a sense, holds true of the baseball fan, who exercises the right to talk to you without knowing you, to shout at you from the stands and to voice his opinion, good or bad, of the play on the field. After all, he is your customer and he feels that you, as a player, and the team, belong to him. Don't let this attitude bother your play. Above all, don't let the remarks of any fans arouse your own ire to the point where you make a scene or display poor sportsmanship.

"Apparently these young women had been instructed that they were expected to maintain the dignity of their sex and American standards of sportsmanship, and so true to the feminine protective instincts, they did. The atmosphere was such that the crowd did not indulge in indignities. . . . On the other hand, if by 'sex' is meant the normal appeal of the feminine mode and attitude then most certainly sex was an important source of interest and a legitimate element of the league's success."

E. W. Moss, *Baseball Blue Book*, supplement no. 9, November 1949

In August 1952, All-American Mary "Bonnie" George Baker appeared as a guest on the popular television game show *What's My Line?*, on which four panelists would attempt to determine a guest's line of work by asking a series of yes-or-no questions. If the guest answered yes, the panelist could ask another question, while a no moved play on to the next panelist; at ten no answers, the guest would win the game. Upon introduction, Baker's occupation was revealed to viewers, and the studio audience giggled with delight as the "professional baseball player" took her seat for questioning. One particular panelist, Hal Block, began a rapid-fire line of questioning that stuck to his presumption that Baker was in a much more risqué line of work.

"Well, I don't know about the 'Baker,' but this is quite a sweet cookie! . . . Oh, you doll! Do you deal in services, Mrs. Baker?"

"Yes, I do."

"Do people come to you?"

"Yes, they do."

"Do you entertain them at all?"

"Yes."

"You do? Do you do your work in front of an audience?"

"Yes, I do."

"Are there ever . . . men in the audience?"

"Quite a few!"

"Really?! Uh . . . do you by any chance do anything *physical*?"

"Yes."

"Do you . . . do you by any chance wear a special costume?"

"Mmhmm."

"In the course of your work, do you ever take part of the costume *off*?"

"Yes."

"And the thing is sometimes scanty? The thing that you wear is—sometimes doesn't cover below your knee?"

"Now this is just the issue of what you have in your own mind, the costume is adequate to its purposes!"

With five allotted no answers down and five remaining, panelist Dorothy Kilgallen surmised Bonnie's profession, declaring, "I certainly think Mrs. Baker is an argument for allowing women to play in the big leagues!"

MR. DALY

"Well, for heaven sakes, I *must* get more interested in baseball."

Bonnie Baker was a skilled catcher and utility infielder from 1943 to 1952, and one of the few female managers in the league, doubling her duties for the Kalamazoo Lassies in 1950. After the league ended, Bonnie went on to become Canada's first female sportscaster in 1964.

MR. DALY

"Men are ardent and vociferous fans, to be sure. The first time they go to the park they are likely to be thinking of bare knees (a masculine failing which is not to be condemned too readily), but after the first inning they have forgotten the knees and are gawking with wonderment at the skill of the fielders, the lusty swings of the batters, the assortment of 'stuff' the pitchers display. But women make the game possible. Housewives and cooks, clerks and secretaries and salesgirls, find a delight which they make no effort to conceal in watching members of their own sex play a game just about as well as their brothers can play it. The spectacle feeds their pride and goes a long way toward dispelling the myth of inferiority, the myth of the weaker sex."

Morris Markey, "Hey Ma, You're Out!," *McCall's*, September 1950

"THE BIGGEST KICK CAROLYN GOT ALL SEASON WAS WHEN SHE CAME INTO ANOTHER TOWN TO PLAY ONE NIGHT AND ON HER WAY TO THE BALLPARK MET A BUNCH OF KIDS PLAYING SANDLOT BASEBALL."
"JUST FOR A GAG, CARY GOT ONE OF THE KIDS TO LET HER TAKE A CUT AT THE BALL."
HEY, FELLAS, HOW ABOUT GIVIN' ME A TURN?
"FOR SOME REASON OR OTHER SHE PASTED IT INTO WYOMING."
TWHACK!

Carolyn "India" Morris was a pitcher in the AAGBBL from 1944 to 1946 and a fashion model in the offseason. In her three seasons with the league, she pitched a total 1.55 ERA (earned run average) in 134 games played, including three no-hitters and a perfect game. She did have a brother.

On a warm June evening in 1944, just days after Allied troops had landed on the beaches at Normandy, catcher Dorothy "Mickey" Maguire was suiting up for a night game when she received a phone call from her mother in Cleveland, Ohio. The army had sent a letter: "Your husband has been killed in action."

Somewhere over Italy, Corporal Thomas J. Maguire Jr. had been shot down and was reported dead. Mickey quietly finished suiting up and took to the field, waiting to inform her teammates of her husband's death until after the game.

The scale of World War II left no one unaffected, and many players had friends and family overseas. The league was fully dedicated to lifting morale wherever it could. Spring training in 1945 was conducted in various army training camps, where exhibition games were played for audiences of outgoing servicemen and wounded soldiers, many of whom became devoted fans. The women did their part to lift morale off the field as well, writing to servicemen and visiting hospitalized vets between games or on the road.

"The real value of the league has been its ability to furnish recreation and entertainment to the workers right in their own backyard."

Racine Journal Times, August 27, 1943

Wrigley's vision of boosting home front morale proved successful. By placing teams in midwestern cities with "large number[s] of industrial plants nearby," Wrigley's nonprofit league provided hard-working citizens with some much-needed recreation. With every team playing six games a week, townsfolk grounded by gas rations and long workdays had ample opportunity for fresh air and fun, all while aiding the war effort: game nights also served as war drives, and ticket proceeds went back into the community.

One of the prominently patriotic wartime events put on by the league also happened to be historically significant in the world of Chicago baseball. The Women's Army Corps (WAC) recruiting rally and the All-Americans All-Star game attracted some seven thousand spectators to Wrigley Field. Per the usual pregame, the players took to the field in star-spangled formation: a V for victory during the national anthem.

Night games were normal for the league, but not for Wrigley Field! As one of the oldest ballparks in the country, Wrigley Field would be the last to install permanent lighting, and Cubs fans would wait until 1988 to see a night game in their "friendly confines." Thus, with temporary lights set up behind the diamond, the All-American Girls Softball League played the very first night game (and the second) in Wrigley Field on July 1, 1943. The following year's doubleheader, however, would be played by teams from the All-American Girls Baseball League, appropriately renamed midway through the 1943 season due to Wrigley's many specialized changes to the game.

"The girls game has undergone more revolutionary changes in the last year alone than any other established sport. And whether the individual sports fan likes it or not, it stands today as the most orthodox of all American sports, because it is baseball. . . . For indeed, if girls baseball is unorthodox, so is all baseball unorthodox."

Don Black, *Racine Journal Times*, September 2, 1948

Evolution of AAGBBL Ball Size* and Pitching Style

1943: 12" Regulation Softball size in 1943

Underhand Pitching

mid-season 1944-1945: 11 1/2"

1946-1947: 11"

Limited to Full Side-arm Pitching

1948: 10 3/8"

Overhand Pitching

1949-1953: 10"

1954: 9" **

* in inches

** Regulation Baseball size

"When they really went to complete overhand pitching, I was home free. I knew all the pitches and they had a lot of trouble hitting off me."

Jean Faut, pitcher, third base, 1946–53. The only known professional baseball pitcher, man or woman, to pitch two perfect games in a career.

Evolution of AAGBBL Basepath Distance (in feet)

1943: 65' (Regulation Softball is 55')

mid-season **1944-1945:** 68'

1946-1952: 72'

1953: 75'

1954: 85' (Regulation Baseball is 90')

"[When] we played with a regular baseball—oh my god, how easy! I mean . . . I could grip that ball, wow—and hit it!"

Catherine Horstman. Career batting average: .286.

Evolution of AAGBBL Pitching Mound-to-Home Plate Distance (in feet)

1943-1944: 40' (Regulation Softball was 35' in 1943)

mid-season **1945:** 42'

1946-1947: 43'

1948: 50'

mid-season **1949-1952:** 55'

1953: 56'

1954: 60' (Regulation Baseball is 60' 6")

"They said that they [increased the base path distance] purposely . . . to try to stop me from running. I didn't know that until I read about it [later], I just kept running. You might as well cut my legs off."

Sophie "Flint Flash" Kurys, second base, 1943–52. Career stolen bases: 1,114.

```
"'Time alone will tell just how far we will grow,'
declared [Rockford coach Eddie] Stumpf. 'For the
present, however, it should not be forgotten that
there may not be major-league baseball in 1944. If
that situation develops, then this girls' league may
move in as replacement at various big-league parks.'"
```

Sid Keener, *St. Louis Star and Times*, April 30, 1943

And grow they did; the four teams of the All-American Girls Baseball League in 1943 brought in over 176,000 sports fans. Wrigley opted to expand the league in 1944 with the addition of two teams, the Milwaukee Chicks and the Minneapolis Millerettes. But the league wouldn't be moving into any "big-league parks."

With Allied forces advancing overseas, victory over the Axis powers was in sight; as the demand for military manpower slowed, the threat of major-league extinction soon dissolved.

Despite his initial ambitions, Wrigley, perhaps assuming that the imminent end to World War II would render women's baseball unnecessary, removed himself from his venture and sold the league to ad man Arthur Meyerhoff, who continued to develop its potential.

Finally, with Japan's surrender in August 1945, the brutal and devastating Second World War came to an end. American troops headed home, factories resumed normal production, and men replenished minor- and major-league baseball teams. Even still, attendance at the All-American Girls' games nearly doubled. It looked as though Meyerhoff's acquisition would be safe going into the fourth inning.

Kenosha Comets 1943–51

Racine Belles 1943–50, moved to Battle Creek

Battle Creek Belles 1951–52, moved to Muskegon

Muskegon Belles 1953

Rockford Peaches 1943–54

South Bend Blue Sox 1943–54

Milwaukee Chicks 1944, moved to Grand Rapids

Grand Rapids Chicks 1945–54

Minneapolis Millerettes 1944, moved to Fort Wayne

Fort Wayne Daisies 1945–54

Muskegon Lassies 1946–49, moved to Kalamazoo

Kalamazoo Lassies 1950–54

Peoria Redwings 1946–51

Chicago Colleens 1948–50 (rookie touring team, 1949–50)

Springfield Sallies 1948–50 (rookie touring team, 1949–50)

The league's structure was in constant motion; executives were always experimenting with ways to establish an identity. Some teams never found a foothold, only lasting a season or two, or were moved to a different city. Others quickly found fan support but just couldn't be maintained. A handful, however, became the heart and soul of their cities and remained a tremendous source of pride for the duration of the league and beyond.

"The importance of the Girls' brand of Baseball has been measured in another way, the significance of which I hope will not be overlooked by those who ought to be concerned. . . . The girls' game produced more sand-lot activity in this city among both girls and boys than any influence of the last 25 years."

E. W. Moss, *Baseball Blue Book*, supplement no. 9, November 1949

"I used to have kids come to me all the time. . . . They would come down and sit on the bench with me, these little kids. If I had a chance to give them a ball I would give them a ball or maybe if we would crack a bat and [it wasn't] too bad, I would say, 'Put a little screw in here and it'll be good and you can still use it,' ya know. They would say, 'Oh boy, Pinky, that's good!'"

Noella "Pinky" LeDuc, pitcher, outfield, 1951–54

The women who had grown up as anomalies playing ball with the boys were becoming hometown heroes, inspiring a whole new generation to play ball—and not simply on sandlots. In its first two years, the league held a tournament to raise funds toward a university scholarship in physical education, to be awarded to a young female recipient for the purpose of promoting "athletics among women for health and recreation." By the end of World War II, several team organizations began supporting local boys' baseball clubs and instituted junior girls' baseball leagues, coaching young girls to play and compete like the All-Americans—a clever resource for training potential future players. The All-American Girls game of baseball was catching on, and it had started to change public perception in the process.

"We had to get out there and prove—wearing dresses and with a name like the Fort Wayne Daisies—that we could play baseball. It wasn't easy, but we did it. People may have come out the first time just for laughs and to see the legs, but they kept coming back—and that was because we played good baseball."

Lavonne "Pepper" Paire, catcher, 1944-53

"Girls baseball, as she is played in the AAGBBL . . . is baseball through and through. For verification, you can ask Max Carey, Leo Murphy, Johnny Rawlings, Carson Bigbee, Marty McManus and a list of other former major-leaguers who now teach, coach and manage the girls of the AAGBBL. . . . Don't ever tell any of them that what these girls play is not baseball in every respect."

Don Black, *Racine Journal Times*, September 2, 1948

One of the more legitimizing features throughout the duration of the league was its ongoing lineup of illustrious managers. When Wrigley began his venture in 1943, he made every effort to ensure that it would be taken seriously. The league scouted the highest-caliber female ballplayers. They were expected to play and behave as professionals and would be paid professional salaries.

But high-caliber athletes required high-caliber coaches, so when the United States entered the war in 1943 and minor-league teams lost so many young players to military service, Wrigley saw another opportunity. He solicited the services of out-of-work minor-league managers, most of whom were former big-league players, including Pirates catcher Leo "Red" Murphy; Hall of Famer and master base stealer Max Carey; four-time National League pennant-winning shortstop and World Series Giant Dave "Beauty" Bancroft; Hall of Famer Jimmie "The Beast" Foxx, the second major-league player ever to hit five hundred home runs after Babe Ruth; and pitcher Bill "Wamby" Wambsganss, the only ballplayer in history to execute an unassisted triple play in the World Series.

They may not have been the main attraction, but Wrigley knew their presence would fill a few seats in the stands. But despite the lure of a hefty bankroll and a first-rate team of executives, some would-be coaches started out unsurprisingly skeptical.

MAX CAREY

JIMMY FOXX
FIRST BASE

"One of the managers—their comments will have to remain anonymous for their own protection—said that with men you know where you stand. Men play ball with their muscles and sometimes their brains; the girls, he said, operate mainly on emotion."

Robert Sullivan, *Sunday News*, July 4, 1948

"Whenever a fan yells out to Peoria Manager Leo Schrall on the coaching line: 'Hey! How can I get a job like yours?' he always yells back: 'Listen, Mac, most men can't handle one woman. How'd you like to have to worry about eighteen?'"

Adie Suehsdorf, *This Week*, July 31, 1949

Donald "Chet" Grant (ironically, an American football player and coach with comparatively minimal baseball experience) went so far as to label the ladies' game "a hybrid travesty on the national pastime," but went on to coach three seasons of it with the league from 1946 to 1948 and authored the league's *Guide for New Managers*. Despite having written guide rules like "11. Keep in mind that a girl, though quick to grasp a baseball idea, is not as likely as a boy to retain it," Grant became an enthusiastic and vocal champion of the All-Americans. Of their level of play, he was known for touting: "You had to see it to believe it, and then you didn't!"

"[Max] Carey and the other old ball players connected with the league are still a little astonished at the success of the thing. They also can't help being a little amazed every time they watch the girls at work, but they are growing less and less amazed as they get used to the idea of running a league with skirts instead of pants. They figure they have got hold of something good."

Robert Sullivan, *Sunday News*, July 4, 1948

"Let's face it, look at society during those years, the men were in charge of everything. Religion, economics, politics, and baseball. There were men managers, the men were the umpires, the men drove the bus. But they treated us as baseball players. That doesn't mean they didn't treat us with respect, they respected us as women. They were very aware that we were women, but as far as the game was concerned, we were treated like ball players."

Lois Youngen

The league managers typically did what great managers do: They assisted individual players in cultivating their game and coached them together into competitive teams. Shortstop Toni Palermo insisted, "It was an advantage [that] we had all these coaches and managers that really taught [us]."

"Max Carey, lemme tell ya, he was by far the best teacher I ever had. He taught me things—the kind of things that make you a total ballplayer—like how to watch pitches so you can get a jump to steal . . . how to bunt, how to bluff a bunt, how to protect runners . . . and sacrifice—I loved to sacrifice!"

Wilma Briggs

"One time I was up to the plate and [Coach Jimmie Foxx] said, 'Did you live on a farm and milk cows?' I thought, 'Wow, does it show?!' He said, 'You got wrist action like a farmer!' . . . I hated to milk those cows and here it was the greatest thing I ever did."

Catherine Horstman

"We were impressed with the idea that you watch your opponents to find out what their weaknesses were. [Coach] Woody [English] would always say, 'Did you see that she couldn't hit a high ball in batting practice?' You learn[ed] how to keep your mouth shut in the dugout and pay attention to what was going on. . . . [The major-leaguers now], they're blowing bubbles . . . making big money. They get caught off base and—I don't want to criticize athletes— but give me a couple million and man, I'll show you stuff."

Mary Lou Studnicka

Coach Bill Allington may not have been a celebrity ball-player, but he was a strong hitter and a bona fide baseball man. Lois Youngen said of Allington, "If somebody cracked open his skull, a little baseball would roll out."

Known for his rule-book pop quizzes and thorough morning meetings, Allington's knack for managing carried him through nine consecutive seasons—more than any other league manager—including four Rockford Peaches championship victories. He even went on to organize a touring team of former league players, Allington's All-American World Champions, after the AAGBBL's demise, thus devoting more than twelve of his thirty-one years in baseball to coaching women. He may have been a tough coach at times, but Allington had great respect for his ballplayers.

"These girls don't know how to take it easy. We get through a nine-inning game in an hour and twenty or thirty minutes. You don't see that in the big leagues."

Bill Allington, coach, 1945-54

"We had very, very enthusiastic fans and in fact, some of them would drive to away games. I don't know where they got the gas, but they got it!"

Jean Faut

"At first we took a lot of ribbing, 'Go home where you belong!' 'Go take care of your kids!' but eventually we won them over."

Vivian Kellogg

"This particular night I was playing right field, so I said to myself, 'Well, I got a runner on third and if that ball's hit to me, I gotta get it in quick because she's *fast*.' So the ball was hit to me and my momentum carried me over the foul line. . . . I made a *bullet* throw and nailed her! You should have heard the crowd, 'Wow! What an arm, what an arm!' . . . That made me feel good. That was good. We had a pretty big crowd that night, too."

Noella LeDuc

"I'm about the only living person that actually saw those women play. . . . They were outstanding. You had no idea . . . nobody in today's world can have an appreciation for the kind of baseball those women played. There was no femininity about the way they played baseball, I'll tell you that right now. There was plenty of femininity after and that stuff. But [when] they were on that ball field it was hard-nosed baseball. . . . It was incredible. It was something you'd never forget."

Bud Daniels, husband of Audrey Haine Daniels

National press always fixated on the femininity of the league, usually scripting gee-whiz stories about the novelty of the teams. But the All-Americans were frequently front and center on their city's sports page. Local sportswriters, who often doubled as scorekeepers, provided spirited game summaries right alongside the box scores, rarely wasting a drop of ink to report on the women's appearance. The games even filled the airwaves. "The 1946 season saw the advent of play-by-play broadcasting," wrote former Blue Sox president Harold T. Dailey, "when Racine radio station WRJN scheduled an elaborate program . . . and direct wire broadcasts of many games." Proud townspeople knew every player by name and number—it was big-league-level baseball in their own backyard. What could be more exciting?

"One game at South Bend . . . they recorded a home run I hit as the longest hit ball at that point in the league. The article in the paper said, 'Marge Callaghan, who is one hundred and some-odd pounds soaking wet, hit the longest ball of the season, and Betsy Jochum is still chasing it!'"

Margaret "Marge" Callaghan, third base, second base, 1944-51

"A true 'world series' in baseball with no international boundaries may soon be a reality. But chances are that when that day arrives, the participants in the series will not be men, but women. There is every indication that the kind of baseball played by girls in the All-American Girls Baseball League will be the vehicle for that 'world series. . . .' Last spring the eight-club All-American Girls Baseball League went to Havana, Cuba, for a three-week training program and series of spring championship games. . . . [It is] already one of the most cosmopolitan groups of feminine athletes in the world, with Cubans, Canadians and all nationalities of Americans."

Publicist Fred K. Leo, AAGBBL publicity release, March 5, 1948

Arthur Meyerhoff and his league president, Max Carey, had far-reaching ambitions for women's baseball beyond the Midwest. On April 20, 1947, some two hundred players and league staff boarded a plane in Miami and headed for Havana. An extraordinary exhibition of spring training exercises in Cuba would kick off Meyerhoff's exploration of his proposed International League of Girls Baseball. Having hardly set foot outside their hometowns before joining the league, the All-Americans would find a whole new world in Havana.

"There was music twenty-four hours a day in Cuba and it was just wonderful. . . . Of course the Cuban men [were] very sexy, very sexy."

Jean Cione

Unfortunately, a Castro-led military coup kept the girls' sightseeing and social activities to a minimum.

"We couldn't go out of the hotel, you know, because it was too dangerous, so . . . it was kind of comical. We had [a] long rope . . . hung from the third floor, and it had a basket on it, and we would lower that— and the guys downstairs would go and get us some Cokes, you know, and we would pull it up."

Joyce Hill, catcher, first base, outfield, 1945–52

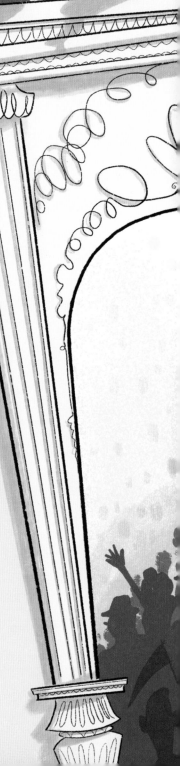

In anticipation of the league's arrival, Havana businessmen organized a Cuban counterpart: the Latin American Feminine Basebol League. Exhibition games between the *Americanas* and *Cubanas* were so popular that organizers quickly orchestrated three consecutive winter exhibition tours throughout Latin America.

"We packed the stands every night; they loved to watch us play and practice!" recalled Jean Faut. *Sporting News* reported, "Cuba is baseball-mad. . . . Games at the end of the training drew tremendous crowds."

"Hundreds turned out to see them practice," recounted Harold T. Dailey, "and no less than fifty thousand wildly enthusiastic fans watched the round-robin tournament."

Base-Ball Femenino
CAMPO ATLÉTICO CHARLES H. TERRY
LUNES 3 DE MARZO 1947
CUBANAS
9:45 am   VS.   3:45 pm
AMERICANAS
★ UNA ESTRELLA EN CADA POSICION ! ★

Enthusiasm surrounding the All-Americans and Cubanas offered "convincing proof that Cuba had taken girls baseball to its heart." The women even drew larger crowds than a better-known group of American baseballers who had trained in Cuba earlier that spring. Wrigley's old friend Branch Rickey and his Brooklyn Dodgers landed shortly after the Cuban League's own pennant race—perhaps the most exciting in its history.

Havana had been a baseball hot spot in 1947, but for the Dodgers, it also provided refuge from the firestorm of threats and negative media that surely would have surrounded them in the States.

That spring in Cuba, a promising new player had joined the Brooklyn roster; a young man with brilliant composure, on and off the field. But Jim Crow was not prepared for Jackie Robinson. Team training facilities were in Miami, and segregated South Florida would not welcome Major League Baseball's first African American star. And while the signing of African American players was never officially forbidden by Major League Baseball, the segregated world of sports was conflicted over Rickey's intent to break the baseball color line. Jackie Robinson's skill and brave decorum would one day define him as a legend, but "baseball people," as Branch Rickey stated, were "slow to change and accept new ideas."

The *Cubanas vs. Americanas* exhibition tours of Latin America would prove so successful that Meyerhoff and Carey quickly recruited several *Cubanas* to the All-American ranks.

"The 200 players on the league's ten teams come from all over the United States and Canada and Cuba and seem to have at least one thing in common-devotion to baseball that is almost religious."

Robert Sullivan, *Sunday News*, July 4, 1948

"Oh my dear . . . my mother . . . she would cry because that was her ideal, the baseball, she loved baseball. She would sit there [in our house] and listen [on the radio] to the Cubans baseball playing. . . . She would light a little candle, she loved baseball. . . . She probably would have liked to play ball herself."

Isabel "Lefty" Alvarez, pitcher, outfield, 1949–54

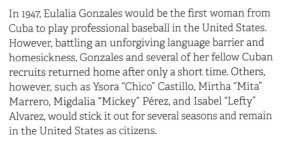

In 1947, Eulalia Gonzales would be the first woman from Cuba to play professional baseball in the United States. However, battling an unforgiving language barrier and homesickness, Gonzales and several of her fellow Cuban recruits returned home after only a short time. Others, however, such as Ysora "Chico" Castillo, Mirtha "Mita" Marrero, Migdalia "Mickey" Pérez, and Isabel "Lefty" Alvarez, would stick it out for several seasons and remain in the United States as citizens.

Lefty Alvarez got her start in the States with the Chicago Colleens, one of two teams newly reestablished in 1949 as a touring "rookie team" (the other team being the Springfield Sallies). The All-American minor-league teams would play one another in exhibition games all over the country, getting in practice while providing the league with plenty of publicity—and sometimes new talent.

"We went to twenty-one states and Canada in three months. And we played seventy-seven games of the ninety-game schedule—we got rained out the rest. We played Yankee Stadium . . . met Joe DiMaggio, Casey Stengel, Phil Rizzuto, Whitey Ford, and all those guys."

Mary Moore

"I left my shoes on the bus, that's how excited [I was] to be in Yankee Stadium. To walk inside for the first time . . . oh my goodness. Yogi Berra asked me if I wanted to use his bat . . . it was a club! . . . If I had picked it up and swung it, I would *still* be going around in circles."

Jacqueline Mattson

"A typical day [was] . . . get up in the morning, have some break-fast, then you walk to the ballpark. Practice at ten o'clock . . . 'til lunch, then you leave and go back to your room and try to get some rest because you gotta be back at the ball field by five. And then you have infield practice, batting practice, then the game starts. I used to think, before I knew better, 'They [have] a nice life—they get to play ball. . . .' But actually, it's a very strenuous job, professional sports."

Jean Faut

Every season, from spring training in April until September, the women of the All-American Girls Baseball League played eight games per week—six nights and Sunday doubleheaders. Only the weather would grant the occasional day off. "Believe me, we prayed for rain," remembered pitcher Dorothy "Dottie" Wiltse. When playing hometown games, the girls would stay with local families, who provided meals, laundry, and all the comforts of home.

But every team spent a good amount of their season in transit, and it wasn't always comfortable, particularly during the war years when gas rations meant the girls traveled by rail.

"We would all be singing,
'Oh we hail from Illinois /
it's just across the line /
we're not too young, we're not too old /
in fact we're in our prime. /
Oh, we hit the ball with might /
in fielding we are fast /
we are the Rockford ball club and we always dress in class /
so we never kick the gong and we're always on our toes /
not only in the ballpark, but when we're with our beaux. /
Oh, we're in bed by ten o'clock /
that is a dirty lie /
we are the Rockford ball club /
a model do or die.'
And we'd be clapping, and I always
remember the words."

Mary Pratt

"When we traveled we didn't have luxury.... Those
were war years, and we often sat in the aisle of
[the] train on top of our suitcases.... Finally they
gave us one of the rickety buses. They couldn't
even find a bus like that for the movie!"

Sophie Kurys

"The one real hardship was that we traveled by bus. Many's the Saturday night that we'd play our ball game, get something to eat, board the bus at twelve midnight, ride all night, get in just in time to go to the hotel, put on our uniforms—some ballparks didn't have dressing rooms—and go out on the field for a doubleheader."

Lavonne "Pepper" Paire

"Some people use to say, 'How did you do it? Those long bus rides and all?' You know, when you're sixteen years old and you're doing something you like to do, that was the least of my concerns, the bus ride. It was fun, it was a lot of camaraderie with the girls, we had good times, we had a lot of laughs. . . . I never minded the bus rides."

Shirley "Hustle" Burkovich, infield, outfield, 1949–51

"There was no complaining, moaning, groaning, and no gossiping. . . . Think of all those women together . . . no air conditioning, you're on the bus, sweltering, clothes hanging in your face drying out, and trying to sleep on the bus, taking turns using one another's laps as head rests, feet up in the air and then switching off—and not being crabby, that's amazing."

Toni Palermo

Morris Markey, "Hey Ma, You're Out!," *McCall's*, September 1950

The following rules will be enforced to the letter by the league and full recourse will be taken against all offenders.

1. ALWAYS APPEAR IN FEMININE ATTIRE. This precludes the use of any wearing apparel of masculine nature. Feminine attire acceptable by general public on the bus and at the beach are permissible. No one will be allowed to appear off the bus in slacks, shorts, or dungarees.

"You could ride on the bus in blue jeans or shorts, but if you got off, you had to put on a skirt, and I mean even at midnight!"

Sue Kidd, pitcher, first base, 1949–54

"We all rolled our jeans up and [would have] our jeans under our skirts. . . . We all looked like we were about two hundred pounds."

Jeneane DesCombes

"WE GOT BACK INTO [GRAND RAPIDS] LATE ONE NIGHT, SO THE NEXT MORNING, EVERYBODY WANTED TO GO OUT TO BREAKFAST, AND WE ALL HAD SHORTS ON."

"[BUT] WE WERE GOIN' ON THE OTHER END OF TOWN, WE THOUGHT NO ONE WAS GONNA SEE US, RIGHT?"

"WELL, LITTLE DID WE KNOW THAT OUR CHAPERONE, DOTTIE HUNTER, HAD A DENTIST APPOINTMENT RIGHT ACROSS THE STREET . . . AND SHE SEES THESE FOUR OR FIVE CHICKS WALK IN THE CODDLE HOUSE IN A PAIR OF SHORTS, WELL . . . I THINK SHE JUMPED OUT OF THAT DENTIST CHAIR! SHE RAN OVER AND SAID,

YOU EAT YOUR BREAKFAST AND YOU GET HOME AND DON'T *EVER* LET ME SEE YOU IN PUBLIC IN A PAIR OF SHORTS AGAIN--YOU PUT ON A SKIRT!

"WE WERE CAUGHT RED-HANDED . . . BUT WHO KNEW SHE HAD A DENTIST APPOINTMENT ACROSS THE STREET?!"

Dolly Niemiec

"You have to understand that we'd rather play ball than eat, and where else could we go and get paid $100 a week to play ball? . . . You wore your hair below your shoulders; you wore skirts and dresses in public. You never wore shorts or slacks in public, and you never smoked or drank in public. We could only date with a chaperone's permission, and we had to be in bed two hours after the ball game. Of course, there were a few little ways of getting around the rules, as long as you were discreet and didn't flaunt it. I've gone down and up many a fire escape, with the coaches sitting right there in the lobby."

Lavonne "Pepper" Paire

"We always had to be in two hours after the game. . . . Well, one night, before we knew it, it was about fifteen minutes past! We go back to the hotel and we look inside, and sure enough, there's Bill [Allington] and the chaperone waiting for us. So, we went around the back of the hotel and the janitor happened to be there, so we says, 'We'll give you five dollars if you don't say anything and let us in!'

"He took us up the freight elevator. Well, pretty soon there was a knock at the door of our room; it was the chaperone. . . . We acted like we were asleep; we snored away like crazy!"

Catherine Horstman and Dolly "Lippy" Vanderlip, pitcher, 1952–54, recalled in tandem; still friends today and still finishing each other's sentences

"[The chaperones] were wonderful; they were really great to us. But we played a lot of pranks . . . like putting limburger cheese on the light[bulbs]."

Helen "Gig" Smith, outfield, 1947-48

"Of course, nobody wanted to admit anything. The next day the chaperone told us, 'It smells just like a dog died in my room last night.' "

June "Lefty" Peppas, first base, pitcher, outfield, 1948-54

Your chaperone is your friend, your counselor and guide. She comes into the All-American Girls Baseball League with a specific assignment and she has her job to do in keeping with her duties and her responsibilities, just as you have your own job to fill. Be helpful, friendly and cooperative with her and do not take advantage of her good nature or her desire to be your friend. She has a direct responsibility to you, to your family, to the club which employs her and to the League which she represents. Adhere to the rules and regulations in a manner that will not reflect upon her. Feel free to go to her with any of your personal problems and you will all derive a greater enjoyment and a finer benefit from your association.

Shirley Burkovich

"The game has been a godsend for some . . .
the ones who are plain and not the mar-
rying type but still have lives to live.
They have gained poise and assurance from
performing before crowds and the knowledge
that they can make use of a talent has done
something for their egos."

Robert Sullivan, "Who Said Girls Couldn't Play Baseball?"
Sunday News, July 4, 1948

"You're talking about the fifties, and the philosophy . . . was that women get married, have kids, and are in the kitchen making meals or working on the farm."

Catherine Horstman

Before the demands of World War II required a "change of duty" in the traditional household, the most socially acceptable—and typical—job for a woman was in the home. Even during and after the war, when women had proven their value otherwise in everything from code cracking to shipbuilding to base stealing, public opinion about a woman's purpose remained unchanged. Throughout the 1940s and 1950s, a woman's value continued to be determined by her ability to marry—a notion that new forms of media would reinforce.

With the expansion of television came the first American sitcom in 1947, *Mary Kay and Johnny*, about a pair of New York newlyweds; it was the first television program to show a couple sharing a bed, as well as the first television pregnancy. Other domestic comedies like *I Love Lucy* and *The Honeymooners* would soon follow. Popular periodicals like *Ladies' Home Journal* also attempted to restore the postwar social order, featuring articles like "You Can't Have a Career and Be a Good Wife" and "Are You Too Educated to Be a Mother?"

The US marriage rate had reached a new high in the 1950s, yet the percentage of single *and* married women earning college degrees and working outside the home continued to climb; social pressures and the propagandized push toward the home were not enough to stall momentum for women in the workplace.

Every woman who played in the league would likely say that they'd have done it for free. "I just went out because I loved the damn game, you know," explained pitcher Noella LeDuc. But the substantial paycheck was a strong incentive and served to legitimize the sport and the women who played it, improving their lives in countless ways. Most of the women sent at least half of their weekly paycheck home to family, who would put it into savings (as one player put it, "ATM: All To Mother").

"You [didn't] have time to spend any money!" recalled Jean Faut. "My first year, I sent fifty dollars to my mother every week. And that was in the '40s! You [didn't] have time . . . no time to go shopping, all you [did was] play ball and catch something to eat every once in a while."

The rigorous season schedules also meant that it was possible to save their earnings, which gave the women access to higher education and other opportunities they would not likely have had otherwise.

League travel offered experiential education and independence, exposing the women to more of the country—and the world—in one season than most Americans had seen in a lifetime. And while roughly 5 percent of American women in the 1950s completed four or more years of college, nearly half of the women who played in the All-American Girls Baseball League went on to earn associates, bachelors, masters, and PhD degrees, becoming educators, physicians, lawyers, administrators, pilots, coaches, and more. But because such endeavors and accomplishments by women were not typical of the time, pursuing ambitions would not always come easy for the players.

"[My] first year in college . . . I was called into the president's office because I was playing ball with a boy on campus. Do you believe that? I was passing ball with a boy on campus, so they called me into the president's office and they said, 'We are not allowed to do that here.'"

Ann Meyer

"It wasn't that my father didn't want the best for me. . . . It wasn't that he didn't want me to do well or have the best of things, but I had a brother, and he was supposed to get all of that."

Delores "Dolly" Brumfield, infield, outfield, 1947–53

"Did [your dad] get a chance to see you play?"

"He probably did, but he wasn't interested in it. Girls should be in the house, you know, and wash the dishes. I'm so *sick* of washing dishes."

Helen "Fil" Filarski, third base, 1945–50

"World War II was the really big one for my generation. . . . Times changed, women had to leave the home and the kitchen. Now that the men are coming back, you women get back in the kitchen! I'm sorry, you've opened the door of opportunity and we're not in the kitchen, we're out in the world being productive and doing other things and having other opportunities."

Delores "Dolly" Brumfield

"The so-called gentle sex has already taken over such he-man pursuits as driving trucks, busses, street cars and taxicabs. They've supplanted us as laborers. They've manned—or wimmened!—the war plants as riveters. They have invaded the halls of Congress, become governors of some of our great States, and have wedged their shapely ways into law and medicine. They've taken up wrestling, even!

But baseball? This can never be!"

Vincent X. Flaherty, "Gal Players in the Majors!," *San Francisco Examiner*, October 15, 1950

"You've got to remember that this was a time when it was not a popular idea for a woman to be playing baseball. We didn't realize what pioneers we were, but we were really out there as forerunners, as far as women's sports are concerned. We constantly bucked public opinion. You know, they looked at you kind of funny and thought maybe you should be in the kitchen, or you should be at home sewing curtains, but you certainly shouldn't be out there running the bases."

Lavonne "Pepper" Paire

The All-Americans certainly bucked public opinion, and sometimes private opinion, too. Dorothy "Mickey" Maguire, who suited up and played her game after learning her husband had been killed in action, received another letter, two months later that summer in 1944—"He's alive."

Tom Maguire had likely lost his dog tags under enemy fire and was presumed dead. As Mickey's son Rick Chapman recounted, upon Tom's return home to Ohio, "Mom's taking care of him and he says, 'You need to quit baseball.' And she says, 'But I make a lot of money playing baseball!'"

A Cleveland cab driver in the off-season and a hard-nosed natural behind the plate, Mickey had been holding her own as a widow. Now, suddenly unwidowed and with an out-of-work husband to care for, it seemed natural that her year-round income would be appreciated.

"Well, evidently it didn't work out," chuckled Chapman. Mickey Maguire went on to play five more seasons of professional baseball, officially divorcing Tom Maguire in 1947 and remarrying to become Mrs. Chapman the following year.

Slicing the idea of "breadwinner" into equal shares was often difficult for men of the time. But married All-American ballplayers typically had supportive husbands who saw their wives' baseball career as a plus.

"Yeah, I was a saver and that was one of the reasons that I could con my husband into letting me play ball! I could save my money, you know, and [he] could save [his] and we [could] add those . . . five rooms [to the house]," recalled Joyce Hill.

"I started carrying that the year we got married, 1948. The summer of 1948 . . . they took individual pictures of the players and I have this picture of her. . . . That's gone through about eight or ten wallets, but I think just the quality of that picture from 1948 is outstanding."

Bud Daniels, husband of Audrey Haine Daniels, who has carried his wife's baseball photo in his wallet every day for over seventy years.

"You won't believe this, but the Fort Wayne Daisies baseball team had a fair chance for the pennant last year until its star pitcher dropped out in mid-season to have a baby. Yes, sir, the pitcher had won 13 and lost eight, struck out 1-1, and compiled an earned run average of 2.01 by July. And then the baby came.

At Rockford, Ill., the Peaches' shortstop last year was Harrell. This season it's Doyle. Two different players? Not at all. Shortstop simply got married. . . . And where can such things happen? Where do matrimony and motherhood make managers wish they had nothing more than sore arms and Charley horses to worry about? They happen in the All-American Girls Baseball League."

Adie Suehsdorf, "Sluggers in Skirts," *This Week*, July 31, 1949

Doctors in the 1940s and '50s were only just debunking the baseless medical assertion that women had a finite amount of energy to spend during their lives, and should any of that energy be expended on rigorous athletics, little would remain for pregnancy. While only a small percentage of All-Americans became mothers during their playing years, they proved they could provide for their families, and that matrimony and motherhood were certainly possible for the professional athlete.

"Dorothy Collins, leading pitcher for the Fort Wayne team, took her regular turn on the mound (with her doctor's approval, of course) until her pregnancy reached the fifth month. Baseball paid for her baby, which was born in the winter, and she was back for the opening of the season without missing a single game."

Morris Markey, "Hey Ma, You're Out!," *McCall's*, September 1950

Blue Sox pitcher Jean Faut married shortly after her first season with South Bend and became a mother just before her second, but neither hurt her playing one bit. Following the birth of her son, Faut posted a 1.44 ERA and batted .231 for the season, and she only got better, leading the league in wins and shutouts in 1949, with a whopping .291 batting average.

Like other wedded women in the league, when Faut wasn't on the field, she carried out all the normal duties of a wife and mother at home. And when the Blue Sox hit the road, her husband, Karl Winsch, would cook, clean, and care for their young son, Larry—that is, until 1951, when their schedules and marriage hit a snag.

In 1951, Winsch, a former minor-league pitcher and Phillies prospect, got a new job—as the Blue Sox coach. Unfortunately, Winsch's career move was not a happy surprise for Faut: "I never knew he was gonna be coach until I got to spring training the first day—it was a complete surprise to me. He never mentioned it, and he had signed the contract six months [prior] already. It was a shock. And it did make a difference."

While he may have been a successful coach, Winsch was not a well-loved coach. Described as strict and punishing both on and off the field, his coaching methods drove an unwelcome wedge between Faut and her teammates, who didn't want to hang around the coach's wife for fear of favoritism or tattling.

But none of it made a difference in Faut's game. Despite unique and isolating pressures, she was named 1951 Player of the Year, a year in which she pitched her first of two perfect games and helped the Blue Sox win the championship.

"You just block everything out, you just concentrate on the game," explains Faut. "That pressure is always there."

That pressure escalated in late 1952, Faut's strongest year.

As the result of an argument, Winsch fired one of his players, and six more walked out behind her in protest, leaving South Bend with a twelve-woman roster going into the playoffs.

"Yeah, we was the 'Dutiful Dozen,' that's what the newspaper said," recalled Mary "Wimp" Baumgartner, Blue Sox catcher. The shorthanded Dutiful Dozen went on to win the 1952 AAGBBL Championship, due in large part to Faut's commanding contributions. She finished that season leading the league in strikeouts, posting twenty wins, two losses, and an astounding 0.93 ERA.

HOME EDITION

The South Bend

SOUTH BEND, INDIANA   FRIDAY, SEPTE

GAME NOTES
By Jack Luke

DUTIFUL DOZEN
SHORTHANDED BLUE SOX WIN AAG

In the end, her husband's derisiveness and the difficulty of his presence on the team just wasn't worth it for Faut. She finished the 1953 season pitching a second perfect game, setting a league record with her 1.23 career ERA, and was again named Player of the Year. Though she would later express regret, Faut did not return for the league's final season.

Jean Faut was one of many exceptional athletes who built a remarkable career as an All-American. Women who played several years often grew stronger as veterans, outdoing themselves with each passing season. Players like Lois "Flash" Florreich, Betsy "Sockum" Jochum, Edythe "Edie" Perlick, and Helen "Nicki" Nicol, had all been signed in the league's inaugural year and would go on to set outstanding individual records, inspired team managers—eight of them at the time—to collectively vote on and assemble the league's first All-Star team in 1946. The team then competed in an exhibition game against the championship-winning team of the season. Selected for outstanding performance, some of the league's strongest players made multiple appearances on the annual All-Star roster.

Sisters Betty and Joanne Weaver collectively appeared on five All-Star teams as a result of their unstoppable bats. In just five seasons each, Betty and Joanne set the league records for first and second highest career batting averages, .349 and .352, respectively. "The [Weaver] girls were farm girls, and when they hit that ball," recalled infielder Margaret Callaghan, "you might as well stand next to the fence because it was going to go out." Their baby sister, Jean, played just three seasons, but all the Weaver sisters were known for their astonishing speed; once, for a pre-exhibition game stunt with Bill Allington's All-Stars, Joanne even raced a horse—and won.

Of course, the most notorious speedsters in the league were also the stealthiest. Five players share the league record for most stolen bases in a single game: an impressive seven. One of those players, four-time All-Star Sophie "Flint Flash" Kurys, also holds the league record for most stolen bases in a season with 201. In her nine years with the league, Kurys amassed a career record of 1,114 stolen bases. "Some of the pitchers, if they didn't pay any attention to me," Kurys remembered, "I could steal their pants off."

If there's anything to a name, theirs could have been synonymous with the long ball: Eleanor "Slugger"Dapkus racked up thirty home runs in her seven-year career, while three-time All-Star Eleanor Callow hit more home runs (fifty-five) and triples (sixty) during her seven seasons than any player in league history. Another heavy-hitting All-Star, Audrey Wagner, hit fifty-five triples in her seven years, and in 1948 earned the title of Player of the Year, an award bestowed on a single player each season.

AUDREY WAGNER

The first All-American to be named Player of the Year, Connie Wisniewski, appeared on five All-Star teams as both a pitcher and an outfielder with a strong bat. As a pitcher, Wisniewski posted the highest career win percentage of any player and holds the league record for most innings pitched in a season (391). The suitably nicknamed "Iron Woman" pitched forty complete games in 1946 and twice in her career won both games of a complete doubleheader.

"Iron Woman" Wisniewski could have shared her nickname with pitcher Joanne Winter, who in 1946 pitched sixty-three consecutive scoreless innings, producing six shutouts; the two women share the league record for most wins in a season (thirty-three).

CONNIE WISNIEWSKI

The 1950 Player of the Year, Alma "Ziggy" Ziegler, "was a truly great ballplayer," remembered Lavonne "Pepper" Paire. "She could beat you with the stick or the mouth or the brains or the hustle." Ziegler started as a strong fielder with an even stronger bat, and also moved to—and excelled on—the pitching mound. It was not uncommon for an All-American to play multiple positions well; in Doris Sams's eight seasons, she appeared on five All-Star teams, four of those appearances as both an outfielder and a pitcher. Though she was one of only two players to twice be named Player of the Year (the other being Jean Faut), Sams insisted she "got lucky" when she pitched a perfect game in 1947, that the opposing Daisies hit off her "like a drum," but her teammates were "on their toes." A consistent career hurler, Sams only got better with the bat, hitting over .300 her last four seasons and setting the 1952 season record for home runs (twelve).

DORIS SAMS

Third in the league for career home runs, Dorothy "Dottie" Schroeder racked up a series of records: best fielding shortstop for three seasons, as well as most career walks, at-bats, and runs batted in, to name a few. Perhaps Schroeder's most notable record is that she is the only woman to have played all twelve seasons of the All-American Girls Baseball League. A mainstay of the league, Schroeder's consistency as a good ballplayer coupled with her genial personality and ideal feminine image also made her a favorite of fans and the media. Schroeder's most evident quality, however, was her love of the game; when the league folded in 1954, she went on to play all three seasons with Bill Allington's touring All-Stars, thus resulting in an impressive fifteen-year career in baseball.

DOTTIE SCHROEDER

Barely fifteen years old when she signed with the All-Americans in 1943, Schroeder became the sort of well-rounded and consistent clubhouse leader typically valued by major-league managers. A 1947 Dayton, Ohio, newspaper reported of Schroeder: "One day last season when he watched her in action, Charley Grimm, manager of the Chicago Cubs, is quoted as having said: 'If she were a boy, I'd give $50,000 for her.'"

By 1950, the All-Americans had fully caught the attention of the professional baseball world, and for obvious reasons. Recurring validation in the media from sportswriters and former major-league players and coaches sparked questions and discussions about the role of women in baseball and the possibility of allowing them into the major leagues.

In a May 1950 interview, the legendary Deadball Era New York Yankees first baseman, Wally Pipp, publicly declared himself a Rockford Peaches fan and went on to label the team's star player, Dorothy "Kammie" Kamenshek, as the "fanciest fielding first baseman I've ever seen, man or woman."

Kamenshek, a seven-time All-Star in her ten seasons and league leader in career double plays (360) and putouts (10,440), was an equally talented offensive player, striking out only eighty-one times in her 3,736 career at-bats.

Pipp's statement quickly prompted the Fort Lauderdale Braves, a Class B professional baseball club, to contact the president of the All-American Girls Baseball League, Fred K. Leo, with a request to buy Kamenshek's contract and sign her to the all-male Florida International League team.

```
"Major league scouts who have watched the husky Norwood, Ohio,
blonde perform for the Peaches have been quoted as saying that
she could make the grade in O.B. [organized baseball]. Dorothy,
a physical education major at University of Cincinnati, thought
so, too; her concern was whether it was the prudent move."
```

Fort Lauderdale News, August 7, 1950

If for no other reason than obvious economics, Kamenshek did not feel the move would be prudent; the Florida team offered her less money than she was making playing for Rockford. She also cited the disadvantages of competing against men "outweighing her by sixty or seventy pounds," and viewed the offer as more of a publicity stunt. Nevertheless, several sportswriters took the offer seriously, interpreting the unprecedented prospect as a threat to "the last impenetrable stronghold of the male animal."

"Things have come to a pretty pass when they talk about letting wimmen into professional baseball . . . it looks bad, men! They're storming the battlements! Why, only a few years ago wimmen thought a batter was something to make waffles out of. But now look! Baseball men are considering a girl named Dorothy Kamenshek as a likely major league baseball prospect! . . . When asked if ladies would be permitted to play pro baseball, Commissioner A. B. Chandler said: There is nothing in the rules to prevent a woman from playing in organized baseball."

Vincent X. Flaherty, "Gal Players In the Majors!," *San Francisco Examiner*, October 15, 1950

DOROTHY KAMENSHEK

While a woman had never set foot in the major leagues, the exclusion of women from organized men's baseball had not been officially stated. But with the rising sentiment regarding women in baseball and the potential consequence that "with dames in it," there might be "absolutely no future whatever for major league baseball," a rule was finally instituted. In 1952, Major League Baseball formally banned women from playing professional baseball at any level within its organization.

A statement from the president of the National Association of Baseball, George Trautman, was published in *Sporting News* on June 23, 1952:

"So as to remove any possible doubt as to the attitude of this office . . . I am notifying all clubs that signing of women players by National Association clubs will not be tolerated and clubs signing, or attempting to sign, women players will be subject to severe penalties. I have consulted [Major League Baseball] Commissioner Ford C. Frick on this matter and he has asked me to express his concurrence in the view that it just is not in the best interest of professional baseball that such travesties be tolerated."

On the same page, an official *Sporting News* editorial response stated:

"Woman's place may not be altogether in the home, and feminine athletes have won distinction in many sports in which they can compete against others of their sex. But as far as Organized Baseball is concerned, woman's place always will be in the grandstand."

"We are not interested in a meaningless competition with men. We are interested in showing a million people a year—and I hope it will turn into two million—that young women can put on a fine ball game all by themselves."

Fred K. Leo, AAGBBL president and commissioner, 1950–52

Wrigley's strategizing had made the league a success and avoided many of the contemporary stigmas attached to women in sports. He and Meyerhoff had given their all to make women's baseball not just palatable but popular, functioning as its own separate sporting spectacle.

Despite the exciting level of play and major-league- caliber athletes, game attendance had gradually declined after peaking at nearly one million in 1948.

"I bought the league primarily to take it off Mr. Wrigley's hands and see what I could do to continue it, rather than just abandon it. If I hadn't been involved very deeply in the advertising agency, I believe I could have built it into a national spectacle, a continuous game," explained league owner Arthur Meyerhoff. "But it got to be too much for me, and I sold it back to businessmen in the various cities in 1950. If it had been picked up by a smart sports promoter, it might have grown, but it got into the hands of local businessmen who didn't have Philip Wrigley's promotional know-how. They were primarily in it for civic purposes—they had fun managing local girls' baseball teams, rather than looking at it from a promotional standpoint and building it. . . . I think that one lesson these gentlemen who took over the league didn't understand was that one must spend money to make it, and, as they eliminated the elements that made the league in the first place, the league deteriorated."

> "Indeed, the one enduring problem of the league is the discovery and development of new players, and that is complicated by the fact this sort of real baseball is played only within the league itself."
>
> Morris Markey, "Hey Ma, You're Out!," *McCall's*, September 1950

Dwindling resources and publicity made player recruitment difficult; while seasoned players were still going strong in the 1950s, they wouldn't be able to play forever.

For the first time, a generation of young girls had grown up watching women play professional baseball, and by the early 1950s, many other women who had also grown up playing baseball were finally aware that the All-American Girls Baseball League existed and that a career in baseball was possible. Unfortunately, many of those women would never have the opportunity to play.

On a bright Virginia spring day in 1953, Mamie "Peanut" Johnson, a young African American woman who had grown up playing baseball with the boys, just like every All-American, showed up for team tryouts with a friend, hoping to make the cut into the league. But as Johnson later recounted, the scouts "looked at us as if we were crazy."

Similar to the unwritten "gentlemen's agreement" that had barred men of color from playing in the major leagues before Jackie Robinson signed with the Dodgers, AAGBBL administration had an internal understanding about admitting African American women. According to notes from a 1951 board meeting, board members were "against the idea of colored players, unless they would show promise of exceptional ability," conceding "that in the event a club did hire one of them, that none of the clubs would make her feel unwelcome."

Johnson and her friend were sent away without a tryout. Few players recall ever having seen any African American women try out, despite Blue Sox manager Karl Winsch's claim: "We had a few blacks try out, but they just weren't as good. If the league tried harder, shook the bushes more, as we used to say, we might've come up with someone."

Mamie Johnson was certainly someone who could have shown promise had she been given the chance. Rather than give up, she took her exceptional abilities elsewhere, becoming one of three women to make history playing professional baseball in the all-male Negro League.

Infielder Toni Stone and pitcher Mamie Johnson were signed to the Indianapolis Clowns in 1953. Stone played through the season with the Clowns and would play one more season with the Kansas City Monarchs before retiring. Utility player Connie Morgan signed in 1954, replacing Stone on the Clowns for one season before retiring.

Unfortunately, record keeping in the Negro League was not as meticulous or accurate as it was in predominantly white baseball, so the precise length of Mamie "Peanut" Johnson's short career remains unknown. Nonetheless, in 2006, over fifty years after the end of the league, Johnson was unanimously voted in as an honorary member of the All-American Girls Professional Baseball League.

By 1954, more than half of the American population owned a television set and an automobile. New and farther-reaching publicity channels were available: baseball games were being televised, and new highway system billboards provided an abundance of new ad space. But, having severely cut their publicity budgets, new league owners did not take advantage of the opportunities that came with postwar prosperity. Wartime gas rationing was a thing of the past and families sought recreation outside of their hometowns. Television was still a relatively new—and newly affordable—medium for entertainment; fans could watch Major League Baseball games in the comfort of their own home. And having lost some of the socially progressive headway of the war, the ideal place for an American woman was again in the home.

Fan attendance for the five remaining teams in the league decreased significantly. On September 5, 1954, the Kalamazoo Lassies defeated the Fort Wayne Daisies in the final game of the postseason and what would end up being the final game of the All-American Girls Baseball League.

"Then came the news that there was to be no more professional girls baseball. It was like a death in the family for me."

Sarah Jane Sands

"I was just getting [into] my prime. . . . I thought it would last forever. . . . I prayed every day that it would last forever."

Catherine Horstman

"Just about the time [I was] ready to be a good strong veteran for four or five more years, four or five more years [weren't] there."

Mary "Wimp" Baumgartner, catcher, 1949-54

About a dozen women would go on to play a few more years of baseball with Bill Allington's barnstorming team, the Allington All-Stars, traveling together in two cars and staging exhibition games against men's and women's teams all over the country. The rest of the All-Americans would have no choice but to move on. Most would continue to participate and compete—often professionally— in other sports available to them, like golf, tennis, bowling, and softball—many playing into their sixties, seventies, eighties, and longer—but their love of baseball never waned.

"You know when you do something competitively and you stop, you *never* lose your competitive spirit—you have to do something to compete, it just doesn't leave you. . . . Doesn't matter what sport you go into, you gotta really work on it, it doesn't just happen, it calls for a lot of practice. But that's the competitive spirit workin' on ya."

Jean Faut

"My children didn't know it, my husband
didn't know it. No one knew it."

Jeneane DesCombes

"Nobody would talk about it because if you said
women played professional baseball and made,
you know, a hundred dollars a week, they'd
think it was a bunch of malarkey!"

Bud Daniels

"My son Bob said, 'You know, I thought every mother could throw a ball like that!' His friends would come over and they'd be throwin' a ball, you know, and I'd get in and start throwin' [with them] and they'd say, 'Oh my god! Your mother can throw!' [He'd say,] 'Yeah, so?'"

Sue Parsons

"When we'd play, [Mom] would give us some pointers, but we just couldn't understand how she *knew* all of that!"

Rick Chapman

While some All-Americans remained in the towns where they had played, many left for college, careers, and families, often landing in places where people knew nothing about the league. And despite having received national attention, recollections of the AAGBBL lived mostly in the midwestern states. What memories remained in the minds of fans rapidly faded.

Civil rights and women's rights movements would shed light on historical inaccuracies and injustices, but even with a growing awareness of women in sports, the majority of Americans remained unaware that a professional women's baseball organization had even existed in their country. To say you had played professional baseball as a woman in the 1940s or '50s would have been met with disbelief.

"I stopped talking about our league for a long time, because whenever . . . someone would ask me how I knew so much about the game, and I'd say, 'Well, I played girls' professional baseball years ago.' And they'd say, 'You mean softball?' I'd say, 'No, I mean baseball.' And they'd do a double take and say, 'You mean softball.' And I'd say again, 'No, I mean baseball.' And after I'd say it about the fourth or fifth time, they'd say, 'You mean . . . base-ball? Like men's baseball? Like with a hardball?' And from the look in their eyes, I could see that they still didn't believe me. You can look 'em right in the eye and say 'baseball,' and they'll look you right back and say 'softball.' Well, you get tired of doing that, and I can't carry my scrapbooks around on my back."

Lavonne "Pepper" Paire

For Paire, the only people who could have possibly understood her experience were the women who also lived it—and who had all had their fill of the "baseball, not softball" back-and-forth. The passing of Title IX in 1972 sparked an unprecedented interest in women's sports history, and thanks to the intensive investigative work of two young women, Merrie Fidler and Sharon Roepke, who had independently become interested in the obscure All-American Girls Baseball League, players began to reconnect.

In 1982, nearly forty years after the league's inaugural season, *Good Morning America* was present to report: "The lobby of the Holiday Inn's Chicago Center resounded with shrieks, giggles, and gasps . . . as one after another, members of the old All-American Girls Professional Baseball League checked in for their first-ever reunion, and recognized each other—after first checking name tags!"

"Just getting back again and being around all the old friends . . . believe it or not it's like I never left after all these years!"

Jerre DeNoble, outfield, 1947

By reuniting and reliving what most of them have described as their "happiest years," the women began to understand the significance of their collective experience. Suddenly there was interest in their past, and together they could make it known that *yes,* they played *baseball,* and there was a place for them in sports history. "This really happened," said Pepper Paire in 1985, "and now, since we've started talking about it again, people are becoming aware that it happened."

In 1988, the National Baseball Hall of Fame in Cooperstown, New York, unveiled its "Women in Baseball" display, honoring many iconic women whose place in baseball history had previously been overlooked and ignored. In its new exhibit, the Hall of Fame paid special tribute to the All-American Girls Baseball League by recognizing every known player, manager, chaperone, and executive. Opening day for the Women in Baseball exhibit saw over a thousand visitors, including one curious filmmaker.

Not long after the league's honorary induction into the Hall of Fame, Penny Marshall began filming *A League of Their Own*. Players were consulted throughout production and invited to participate and appear in various scenes. When the film premiered in 1992, it brought the history of the long-lost league to the general public. As Betsy Jochum put it, "[People] didn't even know we played until the movie came out."

Within weeks, the world knew about the All-Americans.

"The joy [was] momentous, you know, because I had to prove myself all the time. All the time I was proving myself to myself. . . and there isn't anything better than proving yourself to yourself. It gives momentum to what you do, and there's opportunity then to share that."

Jacqueline Mattson

"I don't think anybody [in the league] had any thought of women in the future while we were playing . . . but . . . a good portion of the women have been in sports all of these years in one capacity or another, as teachers, instructors, or coaches. They all have added to [supporting girls and women in sports] throughout their lifetimes."

Jeneane DesCombes

"Well, you had to have confidence, you had to think that every time you walked out on that mound, you walked out on that mound for one purpose, and it was to win that ball game. . . . Athletes cannot perform unless they have that confidence. . . . Some people call it cockiness. . . . Whatever it is, if somebody asks you, 'Are you good?' you say, 'You betchya.'"

Jean Cione

As role models, coaches, mentors, and advocates, the women of the All-American Girls Professional Baseball League have perpetuated, founded, supported, and inspired opportunities for girls, boys, men, and women in sports. As pioneers, they've shared their struggles and rewards, instilling confidence in young players looking to establish their own purpose.

"It's a free country and you [can] just do anything. Nobody can stop you if you don't want them to. Girls can do anything; just turn them loose, that's all you got to say. They're intelligent, you know, and they don't take much guff from anybody anymore. They're raised different today, and it's a different world. Just think, I got to be part of it."

Mary Baumgartner

For players who have made it to any number of the now forty-eight annual All-American reunions, it proves to be the highlight of their year. As the daughter of one player described the gatherings, "It's as if time has never passed, never existed."

"More important than anything we could have done is that friendships have been renewed. New friendships have been made. . . . I know the girls better now than I did when we played ball."

Dorothy "Dottie" Wiltse, pitcher, 1944–48, 1950. Pitched and won four complete games of two doubleheaders seventeen days apart in August 1945. Wiltse passed away in 2008.

In 2019, of the over 600 women who played in the league, approximately 150 are thought to be still living. Each reunion sees fewer familiar faces, and every year, the possibility of another reunion wanes, but the All-American Girls Professional Baseball League Players Association currently remains a tight-knit community of former players and their families, longtime supporters, as well as new fans who share the mission of "preserving the history of the AAGPBL and supporting women and girls all across our country who deserve the opportunity to play 'Hardball.'"

To this day, former players still share their experiences—speaking at schools and fundraisers, signing autographs, and cheering at ball games. Many have been inducted into multiple halls of fame and have been recognized by local, national, and international museums and organizations. They've been honored by Major and Minor League Baseball; a few even throw out a ceremonial first pitch now and again.

"It was [the] dream of a lifetime. Today when I sign a baseball card for kids, I write on it, 'Follow your dreams.' And I tell 'em, 'Do not let anyone tell you that you can't fulfill that dream.' I love baseball so much. And that was my dream. . . . My knees are shot and my hips are shot today, [but] when you get the dream of a lifetime fulfilled, [you're] never sorry. . . . I'd do it again in a heartbeat if I could."

Sarah Jane Sands

"I just know that I loved the game, I always loved it all my life. And I wouldn't take anything if I had a choice of switching from playing ball to something else. . . . I just loved the game. And the All-American League was beautiful."

Jean Faut

For his revolutionary league, P. K. Wrigley required exceptionally skilled ballplayers. To appease the naysayers, they would have to be feminine in image and upstanding citizens with outstanding character. We'll never know what might have come from Wrigley's experiment had it lived on, but its numbers tell the story of an overall success. One look at a player's stats and we can see her extraordinary athleticism; many of the women's individual records are as impressive as any Hall of Famer. But while their numbers are honorable, "it is not the honor that you take with you," Branch Rickey once stated, "but the heritage you leave behind."

The significance of the All-American Girls' legacy is immeasurable.

"I think . . . perhaps that is the greatest legacy of the League, that it presented a model for all of us growing up at that time that we *could* do whatever we set our minds to—because we didn't know that we couldn't. We saw women who were participating in a sport where women had never played before (professionally). We saw those same women go on to become pioneers in physical therapy, medicine, aviation, education, law. We saw some of them become rich, some become famous in other fields, and some dedicate their lives to the poor, to the church, and to humanity. The women who played in the League were not just great athletes; they were the best that this country had to offer in so many ways."

Ruth Davis, South Bend Blue Sox bat girl, 1952–54; signed a contract
to play in the league's unrealized 1955 season.

Afterword

Batter up!

When I started the task of writing this book in 2018, the walls of my cozy workspace in our Oakland, California, apartment didn't exactly reflect the inner workings of a serious author or a historical archivist, but rather resembled the lair of an obsessive wannabe detective attempting to solve an elaborate crime (or commit one). They displayed two years' worth of research, important historical nuggets of information, anecdotal tidbits, and quotes from interviews and newspaper articles, all printed on slips of paper that had been taped, push-pinned, and re-push-pinned in a weeklong process of analog cut-and-paste, until I had finally managed to connect them all, end-to-end, in an exciting narrative. Each satisfying connection answered a question, and I had nothing but great answers from the incredible women I'd had the pleasure to interview. Throughout the process, however, there remained one nagging question that no slip of paper seemed to satisfy: Why has women's professional baseball not reemerged since the All-American Girls Baseball League folded in 1954?

Coincidentally, right about the time I was finishing up my first draft is when I learned about the Women's Baseball World Cup, an international tournament composed of national women's baseball teams. Though it has taken place every other year since 2004, I only heard about the WWC in August 2018 because it was happening for the first time in the United States. Not only was I instantly caught up in the excitement of rooting for Team USA, but I had also found a possible lead on the current state of women's baseball.

Hope for a simple answer vanished when I clicked on an article about the women who played for Team USA and their lifelong, day-to-day adversities. When I reached a section of the article in which one player relayed the frequently frustrating experience of being told what sport she plays and how people always feel the need to correct her when she tells them she plays baseball by saying, "You mean softball." I was stunned. This woman's experience in 2018 was identical to the experiences of every single All-American who had played professional baseball over sixty-five years ago; it was the very sort of conversation that caused the women of the AAGBBL to stop talking about their experience altogether.

A discovery I had hoped would provide me with an answer only propagated more questions, the foremost being: Why was this conversation still happening? I decided to call a few experts, starting with Team USA infielder Malaika Underwood.

Now thirty-seven years old, Malaika played high school baseball on an all-male team, then attended college on a women's volleyball scholarship, earning a master's degree. In 2006, still hungry for baseball in her life, she discovered the USA Baseball Women's National Team by way of a Google search. She trained, tried out, and has played on the team ever since.

"It's automatic; they don't even think about it, it's so ingrained . . . in the way that our culture is set up around these two sports that sometimes people just *can't* get it right," Malaika laughed to me over the phone. "Even people who have seen me play. Sometimes I just throw my hands up and say, 'I'm not going to win this battle, I'm moving on now.'" She continued on to tell me the "baseball-not-softball" conversation "is a shared experience. I can almost guarantee that every girl or woman who has played baseball has had that happen to them at least once, probably more than that."

To be clear, not a single baseball player I have interviewed—former or current—thinks of softball as some sort of inferior version of baseball, and that's because it is not. Softball is an entirely different sport from baseball. "Especially at the collegiate level," Malaika told me. "Those girls are unbelievable!" The level of athleticism in women's softball and its progression as a sport is a testament to the grit, talent, and growing popularity of women's sports today. The growth of women's softball, however, "if we're going to be frank," Malaika informed me, "impacted the potential growth of girl's and women's baseball."

Which led me to the question of how this came to be. How did two very different sports not only become "the same" in the United States, but when and why were they assigned genders? The short answers to these questions in order are: Little League; 1974; as a way to avoid an avalanche of impending discrimination lawsuits. It's an interesting and infuriating story, the entirety of which I will not relay here, but suffice to say, as the result of a lawsuit filed on behalf of a little girl named Maria Pepe, who wanted nothing more than to play the sport she loved and was very skilled at, the Little League Baseball organization—which had dug its cleats into the dirt and fought hard through the legal proceedings to keep girls off its diamonds— lost the battle and was ordered to allow girls to play. Therefore, it is no coincidence that the same year, 1974, Little League Softball was established as a way to usher girls to a separate field and a whole different ball game. And while the official rules of Little League currently allow girls to play baseball and boys to play softball, a visit to their website clearly and immediately establishes the status quo.

"I can't think in my mind of a sport that has that same issue," Malaika puzzled over the phone. Neither can I. We both grew up in the 1980s and 1990s as direct beneficiaries of the landmark 1972 Title IX federal civil rights law:

No person in the United States shall, on the basis of sex, be excluded from participation in, be denied the benefits of, or be subjected to discrimination under any education program or activity receiving Federal financial assistance.

Malaika benefited perhaps more directly than I did; my athletic capabilities in no way contributed to furthering my education and vice versa. But in my high school years, I discovered a love for individual sports like snowboarding and surfing—a discovery I might never have made without the introduction of professional female boardsport athletes in the 1990s like my heroes, snowboarder Tara Dakides and surfer Lisa Andersen. They blazed trails of acceptability through a male-dominated scene, and just look at their respective sports today! Pretty much every women's sport in America has seen significant growth—many flourishing into successful leagues and industries—since the enactment of Title IX. This is not to say the playing field has been leveled, nor has it been an easy road for any of them, but the incremental and generational changes in women's sports have now established a presence, and many young girls today see athletics as an available option without having to think twice. And while growth for women's baseball experienced arrested development with the advent of Little League softball, there are women in recent history whose tenacity has resulted in new opportunities for change.

My next phone call was to Ila Borders. Now a firefighter in Oregon, the former left-handed female pitcher had a nearly four-year career in men's professional baseball. Ila is the source of many baseball firsts, the most notable being that she is the first woman to have earned a men's collegiate baseball scholarship, the first woman to have pitched in a US men's college baseball game in 1994, and the first woman to start a men's professional baseball game. Ila declared to her father at an early age that she wanted to pitch baseball, and with his support, she stuck with it. When the baseball coach at a prospective high school made it very clear that no girl would ever play on his team, she began to search for an opportunity to play.

"That's all I'm looking for. I'm not saying you have to take me," she told prospective coaches. "I'm just saying give me an opportunity and if you see that I can win ball games, let me play." From that moment on, Ila explained that for every ten people who told her no, there was always one yes, and the key to her persistence was that she "really tried to focus on the people that said yes. As long as I kept my focus on the people that were supportive or the ones that said yes, I was okay."

Another key to Ila's perseverance as a pitcher was her realistic understanding and willingness to work with her strengths. "I'm 5'9", 145 [pounds]. You know . . . a 6'4", 220-pound guy, they're going to throw the ball harder, so you've got to hit spots, you've got to change speeds, you've gotta be deceptive and then you've got to be smart," she explained. "Mechanical stuff, you could get that from anybody . . . you need to know the game."

"For women, it's more of a mental game," explained up-and-coming young baseball player Beth Greenwood. "When I'm playing, it's like, I'm just much more aware of what's happening because I have to be. I have to make up for it."

Wanting to know what a future baseball career looks like for someone following in the footsteps of modern day trailblazers, I reached out to Beth for her perspective. Beth started college in 2019, and while she has undoubtedly benefited from the opportunities forged by women like Ila Borders and Malaika Underwood, her experience has not been without its difficulties. In 2017, an opposing men's team in North Carolina refused to play unless the six women on her fifteen-person co-ed team sat out the game on the bench. In fact, staying off the bench was always a challenge for Beth. After she and the only other girl on her Little League team spent several inexplicable weeks on the bench, she volunteered to catch the most feared eight-year-old pitcher on her team—a position no one wanted—just to get on the diamond.

And in high school, Beth made the varsity team but spent a good amount of time on the bench. This is when the high school girls' softball coach, seeing that Beth was clearly frustrated, approached her and encouraged her to switch to softball, where she could be the starting catcher and have a shot at a college scholarship. "It was hard to say no," Beth confided. "It's just, it [wasn't] baseball and not what I do. They were offering me scholarships for a sport I've never even played—I've never thrown a softball. . . . It's just two different sports."

Beth continues to play baseball, but her experience, I learned, is typical. For reasons explained above, a young girl most often starts with softball, or if she starts with baseball, she "can either be the first and/or only girl on her high school baseball team," explained Malaika, "or she can join her friends on the softball team and potentially go to college. What looks more appealing to a twelve- or thirteen-year-old girl and her parents?"

So, for girls who prefer baseball and are willing to forgo more abundant opportunities (and perhaps more fun) to be the only girl on their high school team, where do they go from there?

"They go straight from high school baseball and into softball for four years and then they try to make the women's national team with baseball and, *gosh darn*," lamented Ila, "there needs to be that college part, too, where we can develop women's baseball players in college and then bring it to a professional level."

"It is no secret if you ask any girl or woman who has had to prove themselves above and beyond in order to get to the same place as a boy or a man on the baseball field, it can be frustrating," Malaika said. "You feel this additional pressure to be perfect in a game that's not perfect."

Having played alongside boys and men for several years, and now women for the past twelve, she says that "playing without that constraint is really freeing." When girls can play with other girls, there is less pressure to be perfect, and "the struggle doesn't feel so lonely."

Providing opportunities for young girls to compete and play baseball alongside one another is a large part of the mission of Baseball For All, a nonprofit organization founded by Justine Siegal, PhD. Apart from her rich academic background, Justine is also familiar with baseball "firsts" and has herself accumulated quite a list. In 2009, she became the first woman to coach a professional men's baseball team. Two years later, Justine became the first woman to throw batting practice to a Major League Baseball team, and in 2015 she became the first female coach to be hired by a Major League Baseball team. But when it comes to personal "firsts," Justine explained that "it's an honor to make history, but it's more important that we build a better future. . . . Being a first is incredibly difficult and mind-blowing and sometimes makes you want to not get out of bed, but . . . it's also incredibly rewarding because you are building that pathway for the girls behind you."

While she continues to make history with her organization, she works with volunteers and organizations like Team USA and Major League Baseball to build as many pathways as possible for girls who want to play, coach, and lead in baseball, because "I mean—girls are everything, right?"

But perhaps one of the most important pathways being built by the organizations creating these opportunities is the pathway that serves as a bridge—a bridge across time, to be specific. Beth Greenwood has been involved with Baseball For All since elementary school. At an event in 2013, she met former All-Americans Shirley Burkovich and Maybelle Blair, who told her about their experiences playing professional baseball in the 1950s. Too young to remember the release of *A League of Their Own*, Beth recalled the experience of meeting Shirley and Maybelle and learning about "this whole thing that people just don't even know happened, and it's an incredible thing that happened. . . . I would always dream that there could be a league, but [didn't know] that there *had* been a league. So it *is* possible. It was kind of like this dream that maybe someday it could happen . . . [but] it *has* happened. So there's no reason why it couldn't happen again."

The importance of understanding that something which feels impossible is actually possible, that it has happened before, is really all most people need to unlock their potential, in sports or otherwise. As Beth astutely noted, "It's more than just baseball."

The year 2018 marked the seventy-fifth anniversary of the All-American Girls Professional Baseball League. The former players, all in their eighties and nineties (and hundreds!), who continue to share their knowledge, enthusiasm, and stories with young girls and women wondering if they will ever have a chance to play in Major League Baseball or if it will ever be possible to have a league of their own, are living proof that it is possible.

It has been such a privilege to sit with some of the greatest women in baseball history. Each of the AAGPBL player reunions I've attended has provided me with the experience of a lifetime. And I'm incredibly lucky to have had so many questions answered by women like Malaika Underwood, Ila Borders, Justine Siegal, and Beth Greenwood. If you're anything like me, however, your questions will likely never stop, and I think that's a good thing. If you would like to learn more about the incredible women of the All-American Girls Baseball League, or if you would like to know more about girls' and women's baseball currently, pages 156 and 157 of this book contain just a few resources to get you started. I hope they will encourage you to seek out further resources.

Never stop asking questions, and as my dad always tells me, keep swingin'.

Players from the Chicago Colleens and Springfield Sallies posed in front of their bus, 1949. Players photographed, from left to right: (on bus) Arlene Kotil, Jo Sindelar, Norene Arnold (partially concealed), Lois Bellman, Barbara Berger, Sue Kidd, Anna O'Dowd, Betty Francis, Toni Palermo, Barbara Payne, bus driver Walt Fidler, (standing) Shirley Danz, Gertrude Alderfer, Lillian Shadic, Frances Janssen, Helen Walulik, Mary Baumgartner, Islabel Alvarez, Pat Barringer, Norma Whitney.

The Cubanas girls team offering flowers to AAGBPL and Cubanas player Isabel "Lefty" Alvarez, while manager Dave Bancroft looks on, year unknown.

Springfield Sallies player Renae Youngberg waits for the ball as Chicago Colleens player Joan Sindelar reaches the bag, 1949.

Joyce Hill Westerman slides into third base, circa 1945–1952.
(Second player and umpire unidentified.)

Sophie "Flint Flash" Kurys slides for home while pitcher Josephine "Jo" Kabick attempts to tag and catcher Joyce Hill Westerman and unidentified umpire look on, circa 1945–1947.

Kenosha Comets player Audrey Wagner greets four young spectators, circa 1943–1949.

Grand Rapids Chicks Lavonne "Pepper" Paire and
Inez Voyce, circa 1948–1952.

Grand Rapids Chicks players Inez Voyce, Alma Ziegler, and Mildred Earp reading a letter while waiting with
their luggage to start a road trip, circa 1947.

Grand Rapids Chicks players Twila "Twi" Shively, Inez Voyce, Ruth "Tex" Lessing, and Connie Wisniewski with their manager, John "Johnny" Rawlings, circa 1947.

Two All-American Girls Professional Baseball League teams stand in the "V for Victory" formation before a game during World War II, circa 1943–1945.

SOURCES:

General history and some quotes, including the quote from Ruth Davis:

Merrie Fidler, *The Origins and History of the All-American Girls Professional Baseball League* (McFarland, 2015).

General history:

All-American Girls Professional Baseball League Players Association: www.aagpbl.org

Norman Hathaway and Dan Nadel, *Dorothy and Otis: Designing the American Dream* (Harper Design, 2014).

Society of American Baseball Research: www.sabr.org.

Primary source materials:

Hesburgh Libraries Department of Special Collections at the University of Notre Dame.

All player statistics, player records, and league records:

W. C. Madden, *The All-American Girls Professional Baseball League Record Book: Comprehensive Hitting, Fielding and Pitching Statistics* (McFarland, 2015).

All quotes from Lavonne "Pepper" Paire, Shirley Jameson, and Arthur Meyerhoff:

Jay Feldman, "All but Forgotten Now, a Women's Baseball League Once Flourished," *Sports Illustrated*, June 10, 1985.

Quote from Rose Folder, page 43:

Jim Sargeant, *We Were the All-Americans: Interviews with Players of the AAGPBL, 1943-1954* (McFarland, 2013).

Quote from Mamie Johnson, Page 124:

Eugene Meyer, "A True American Athlete," *The Washington Post*, February 3, 1999.

All photos on pages 149 to 153 courtesy of the National Baseball Hall of Fame and Museum.

All or partial interview material and quotes by the following individuals provided by Grand Valley State University Special Collections and University Archives Veterans History Project:

Isabel Alvarez

Louise Arnold

Mary Baumgartner

Maybelle Blair

Delores Brumfeld

Shirley Burkovich

Jean Cione

Bud Daniels

Jerre DeNoble

Jeneane DesCombes

Helen Filarski

Joyce Hill

Marilyn Jenkins

Betsy Jochum

Vivian Kellogg

Sue Kidd

Sophie Kurys

Noella LeDuc

Jacqueline Mattson

Ann Meyer

Mary Moore

Toni Palermo

June Peppas

Grace Piskula

Mary Pratt

Helen Smith

Mary Lou Studnicka

Norma Whitney

Lois Youngen

All quotes by the following individuals were sourced from newspaper articles:

Dorothy Kamenshek

Doris Sams

Dorothy Wiltse

All or partial interview material and quotes as well as league history and information provided by the following individuals and obtained from interviews with the author, who wishes to thank them sincerely:

Ila Borders

Wilma Briggs

Shirley Burkovich

Margaret Callaghan

Rick Chapman

Bud Daniels

Lillian Faralla

Jean Faut

Eileen Gascon

Beth Greenwood

Audrey Haine

Catherine Horstman

Betsy Jochum

Joan Knebl

Eleanor Moore

Mary Moore

Esther Morrison

Dolly Niemiec

Toni Palermo

Sue Parsons

Sarah Jane Sands

Justine Siegal

Malaika Underwood

Dolly Vanderlip

Inez Voyce

FOR MORE INFORMATION:

All-American Girls Professional Baseball League Players' Association: www.aagpbl.org

Includes league history, player history, bios, and stats, as well as links to resources like museums, libraries, archives, and halls of fame.

Grand Valley State University Veterans History Project: https://gvsu.edu/vethistory/

All-American Girls Professional Baseball League Oral History Video Interviews.

Baseball Hall of Fame in Cooperstown: 25 Main Street, Cooperstown, NY 13326; online at https://baseballhall.org

Baseball For All: www.baseballforall.com

Nonprofit organization providing meaningful opportunities for girls in baseball.

American Girls Baseball: An affiliation of the All-American Girls Professional Baseball League Players Association.

The mission of American Girls Baseball is to provide a pathway for the development of girls' baseball skills by creating new programs and supporting those which presently exist.

International Women's Baseball Center: www.internationalwomensbaseballcenter.org

Nonprofit with a dedication to "protect, preserve, and promote all aspects of women's baseball, both on and off the field. We strive to inspire the next generation of players by helping them realize their dreams not only of participating in the sport, but also of passing on all they will learn and achieve for generations to come."

WISE (Women in Sports and Events): www.wiseworks.org

The leading voice and resource for professional women in the business of sports.

Trailblazer Series: www.mlb.com/trailblazer-series

Established in 2017, an annual baseball tournament for girls, launched by USA Baseball and Major League Baseball, taking place around Jackie Robinson Day weekend.

USA Baseball Women's National Team: www.usabaseball.com/team-usa /womens-national-team

The New York Yankees and Boston Red Sox are currently the only Major League Baseball teams hosting annual Fantasy Camps for women: www.mlb.com /yankees/fans/fantasy-camp and www.mlb.com/redsox/fans/fantasy-camps.

Stay tuned for **Throw Like a Girl**, a documentary by Cami Kidder
"A feature-length documentary about women striving for acceptance in the game of baseball." www.throwlikeagirlmovie.com

The BASE

The BASE operates a powerful urban academy that combines sports and educational opportunities, shining a spotlight on the limitless potential of our young people, on and off the field. www.thebase.org

ACKNOWLEDGMENTS:

First and foremost, I would like to thank my family for ensuring and perpetuating the laughter, love, story, music, integrity, and sometimes baseball that is the core of our being and operation; I am ever grateful for their support. Thank you to Marlene Orrock for being the first and most devoted female baseball fan in my life and the best hot chocolate buddy. Thank you, Ray Orrock, for being everything I am proud to come from and grateful to be. Thanks, Mom, for being proud of everything I do, for your undying, enthusiastic support and letting me know there are no limits. Thank you, Dad, for knowing me, giving me the tools to navigate, and always helping me to find my own way, in life and in the air.

And to my best pal and partner, Ray Jacildo, for understanding me, encouraging me, and providing unending love, hugs, beautiful music, and clean dishes. Thank you for working hard for us and bringing your talents to the masses, and thank you for my noise-canceling headphones.

A very special thank-you to the greatest voice and storyteller in baseball, my dear and generous friend Mr. Jon Miller and his immeasurably wonderful wife, Janine, without whom, I can safely say, I might have never found the pathway to the best possible career and life adventure.

From the bottom of my heart, thank you to all of the former All-American baseball players who took the time to speak with me and share their stories, and to their wonderful family members for their assistance and their sharing. Thank you also to the family members of players who have passed on for continuing to share their stories, legacies, and photos.

Sincerest thanks to league historian Merrie Fidler. Without your research, work, help, guidance, encouragement, and time, this book would not be possible. And thanks to all of the wonderful, dedicated members of the All-American Girls Professional Baseball League Players Association, many of whom have devoted much of their lives to preserving, promoting, and protecting the legacy of the league and caring for its players and their families. Thank you for welcoming me and allowing me to partake and share in such a special experience.

Endless gratitude for my manager and counsel, Donna Cohen: survivor, mentor, advocate, example, and educated fellow baseball nut whose guidance is positively invaluable and whose belief in me has inspired me to believe more in myself.

To the amazing Julia Patrick of Chronicle Books, thank you for taking a chance on me and for providing me with the most valuable creative experience I could ask for. Thank you for listening, for seeing what I see, and most importantly, for providing me with the insight and tools to elevate my work and make everything I've done so much better. And tremendous gratitude to the team of incredible women at Chronicle Books for not simply making this book a reality, but making it a better reality than I could have ever imagined: Freesia Blizard, Natalie Nicolson, Maggie Edelman, Alison Petersen, and April Whitney, as well as copy editor Elizabeth Berg.

Thank you, Jean Afterman, for your friendship, encouragement, leadership, and contribution to this book. You are an inspiration in every way.

Thank you to Jessica Hische for friendship, donuts, power rocks, and for contributing your awe-inspiring talents to this book; because of you, people who see this on a shelf will want to pick it up.

Very special thanks to James Smither and Janet Coryell of the Veterans History Project at Grand Valley State University and to former curator George Rugg and the welcoming staff of the Hesburgh Libraries Department of Special Collections at the University of Notre Dame. The work you have done to preserve the legacy and history of the league and your generosity in sharing it are priceless and so appreciated. And tremendous thanks to the following people and organizations whose work and generosity greatly contributed to this book: Penny Marshall; W. C. Madden; Jay Feldman; Jim Sargeant; Leslie Heaphy; Dr. Kat Williams; Lena Park; Eugene Meyer; Ila Borders; Justine Siegal; Beth Greenwood; Malaika Underwood; the Society of American Baseball Research; the Baseball Hall of Fame in Cooperstown, New York; The History Museum in South Bend, Indiana; and Midway Village Museum in Rockford, Illinois.

Additional thanks to the friends, creative compatriots, and teachers whose advice, adventures, wisdom, friendship, experience, lessons, laughter, and conversation have provided endless comfort and creative motivation throughout the process: Angela Alaura, Deanna Marsigliese, Bob Peterson, Peter Emmerich, David DePasquale, members of the JD McPherson Band, Mary Moyer, Jeri Larsen, Chris Sasaki, and John Clapp. And thanks to the teachers who, despite my insistence on drawing my way through school and life, encouraged me to continue writing and nurture the joy in it: Jill Lemmon, Cate Munch, and Michael Mangin.

Thank you to friends Abby Benedetto and Jen and Dan Auerbach for facilitating and providing comfortable, quiet places and situations that allowed me to create and write this book. And to the Smay family for being home away from home.

Thanks to Dave Koch, who opened, owned, and operated the Cartoon Factory animation art gallery in Salt Lake City, Utah, in the early 1990s, wherever you are. You set up shop in a time and place nontypical to the rest of the world, but critical for me.

To the countless illustrators, cartoonists, artists, and designers from whom I learned the art of visual storytelling and the value of emotion over technical skill, thank you.

Thank you Roger Angell, Roger Kahn, Ring Lardner, and Ray Orrock for introducing me to the narrative heart and soul of baseball, inspiring me to combine my loves and showing me how it's done.

Thank you, Lefty O'Douls at 333 Geary St. Rest in peace.

Thank you to anyone and everyone in this world who has worked in any capacity to put a good cup of coffee by my side. Thank you to the wonderful Django Reinhardt and Colemine Records for creating catalogs of perfect music to work and draw to. Thank you, Darren Chan and KNBR, Dave Flemming, Jon Miller, Mike Krukow, and Duane Kuiper for baseball on the radio.

Thank you to Carl Reiner and anyone who ever had anything to do with the *Dick Van Dyke Show*, *Mary Tyler Moore Show*, and *Cheers*—the best classrooms ever. And to Roz Chast, Liza Donnelly, Kristen Wiig, and all the ridiculously brilliant and honest female humorists, cartoonists, and visual storytellers who have paved the way; by simply being, you have encouraged me to do my best work and be me.

Thank you everyone and anyone who follows me on social media and generously takes the time to comment or message me with kind words. Last but not least, my humble gratitude to everyone and anyone who has purchased or commissioned my art or my books (thank you San Francisco Giants organization, Mario Alioto and Becky Fenton of the Gotham Club, and Marty Lurie and the Mavraedis's!) or has displayed, promoted, or in any way whatsoever supported my work; you allow me to live in a constant state of gratitude and creativity; you are everything.

photo by Raynier J. Jacildo

ABOUT THE AUTHOR:

Anika Orrock is an illustrator, cartoonist, designer, writer, humorist, archivist, and baseball devotee. Her work has been commissioned by the National Pastime Museum, Merrill Lynch, New West Records, the International Women's Baseball Center, the All-American Girls Professional Baseball League Players Association, Major League Baseball organizations, and international sports publications. Passionate about the history and current role of girls and women in baseball, she has enjoyed collaborating with organizations to educate and promote the advancement of girls in all areas of the sport. Anika currently lives in Nashville, but left her heart in San Francisco.

Jean Afterman is Senior Vice President and Assistant General Manager of the New York Yankees baseball organization. She is the third woman in Major League Baseball history to hold the position (appointed in 2001) and is currently the only woman holding the position. A native San Franciscan, Afterman is also an accomplished lawyer, actress, and art history expert.